HUMAN
RESOURCE
MANAGEMENT

To my daughter Clare Youngs
who designed the book jacket.
Also to my grandchildren, Milly and
Florence Youngs and Charlie
and Lucy Price.

HUMAN RESOURCE MANAGEMENT

STRATEGY & ACTION

MICHAEL ARMSTRONG

KOGAN
PAGE

This book is a completely revised and reworked edition of the author's former title *A Handbook of Human Resource Management* published in 1988.

First published 1992
Reprinted 1993 (twice)
Second Reprint 1994
Reprinted 1995
Reprinted 1996
Reprinted 1997
Reprinted 1998
Reprinted 1999

Kogan Page Limited
120 Pentonville Road
London N1 9JN

© Michael Armstrong 1992

British Library Cataloguing in Publication Data

A CIP record for this book is available from the British Library.

ISBN 0 7494 0714 X

Typeset by Saxon Printing Ltd, Derby
Printed in England by Clays Ltd, St Ives plc

Contents

Preface

Although 'human resource management' is a phrase which has been in use for over 40 years, it did not come to the fore as a distinctive approach to managing people until the mid 1980s, when it became generally known as 'HRM'.

HRM can be defined as a strategic, coherent and comprehensive approach to the management and development of the organization's human resources in which every aspect of that process is wholly integrated with the overall management of the organization.

HRM is essentially an ideology. It is underpinned by a philosophy which starts from the belief that organizations exist to deliver value to their customers, and that this is best achieved by adopting a longer-term perspective to the management of people and by treating them as assets rather than merely as variable costs. HRM sees people as valuable resources for the achievement of competitive advantage who should therefore be managed and developed to their full capacity and potential.

The emphasis in HRM is on the common interests of management and the workforce in the success of the business. It is concerned with the creation of a positive culture and with enlisting the commitment of all employees to the goals and values of the enterprise.

A holistic view is taken in an HRM system of the management of people. HRM adopts an internally coherent approach to personnel practices which are designed to be mutually reinforcing. The emphasis is on strategic integration – matching HRM strategies to the business strategy.

Perhaps the most distinctive feature of HRM is that it is a strategic activity run by management. As Hendry and Pettigrew (1986) stated: 'It is the value diffused through the management system as a whole which gives any set of HRM policies its coherence'. HRM is owned and driven by top management, and line managers are totally responsible for its performance and delivery.

Personnel directors and managers, however, still play a major part in this process. They intervene as necessary with proposals for innovations in human resource policies and practices. They ensure that HRM systems are coherent, facilitate their introduction and see that they function properly. They are enablers, acting as internal consultants; counselling and coaching managers. They are change managers; advising on and helping with the smooth introduction of change. Finally, and importantly, they use their expertise and perception to interpret the needs of both the business and its employees in order to assist with their integration. HRM is indeed the responsibility of management, but without the expert guidance and support of personnel specialists, it is most unlikely to function effectively.

HRM is about process – the ways in which organizations get things done through people – in other words, culture in action. It is not just a bundle of personnel techniques. A comprehensive HRM system is developed at corporate level where the main concerns are the integration of business and HRM strategies, organization and culture management. This system is operated by means of a number of related processes: managing change; creating commitment; achieving flexibility; improving teamwork; and total quality management. These processes underpin the interrelated activities which make HRM happen: resourcing; performance management; human resource development; reward management; and employee relations.

This book considers all these aspects of HRM. It is divided into four parts, the first of which examines the concept of HRM – its philosophy, aims and features, the reservations expressed by some commentators about it, and how it relates to personnel management. The next three parts deal in turn with the three aspects of HRM referred to above: its operation at corporate level; its processes; and the interrelated activities which convert its philosophies into action.

Part I

The Concept of Human Resource Management

Chapter 1

The Basis of Human Resource Management

DEFINITION

Human resource management (HRM) can broadly be defined as a strategic and coherent approach to the management of an organization's most valued assets – the people working there, who individually and collectively contribute to the achievement of its objectives for sustainable competitive advantage.

As described by Beer *et al* (1984):

Human resource management involves all management decisions and actions that affect the relationship between the organization and employees – its human resources.

A further definition is provided by Pettigrew and Whipp (1991) who suggest that:

Human resource management relates to the total set of knowledge, skills and attitudes that firms need to compete. It involves concern for and action in the management of people, including: selection, training and development, employee relations and compensation. Such actions may be bound together by the creation of an HRM philosophy.

The emphasis is, therefore, first, on the interests of management, secondly, on adopting a strategic approach, thirdly, on obtaining added value from people by the processes of human resource development and performance management and, finally, on gaining their commitment to the objectives and values of the organization.

Human resource management can be regarded as a 'set of interrelated policies with an ideological and philosophical underpinning' (Storey 1989). The basic definitions given above need to be supplemented by an analysis of this philosophy.

HRM PHILOSOPHY

The first statements of HRM philosophy were made by a number of

American academics writing in the 1980s. For example, Tichy, Fombrun and Devanna (1982) stated that:

> The long-run competitiveness of American industry will require considerably more sophisticated approaches to the human resource input that deal with its strategic role in organizational performance ... and the strategic human resource concepts and tools needed are fundamentally different from the stock in trade of the traditional personnel administrator.

They suggested that the 'psychological contract' between management and employees should offer 'challenging meaningful work in return for a loyal, committed and self-motivated employee'. They emphasized the need to:

- devise an organization-wide selection and promotion system which supports the business strategy;
- create internal flow of people to match the business strategy;
- match key executives to the business strategy;
- commit managers to weighing human resource issues with the same level of attention as they give to other functions such as finance, marketing and production.

The influential Harvard School, as represented by Beer and Spector (1985), expressed its philosophy as follows:

> We believe that a set of basic assumptions can be identified that underlie the policies that we have observed to be part of the HRM transformation. The new assumptions are:

- proactive system-wide interventions, with emphasis on fit, linking HRM with strategic planning and cultural change;
- people are social capital capable of development;
- coincidence of interest between stakeholders can be developed;
- power equalization is sought for trust and collaboration;
- open channels of communication to build trust and commitment;
- goal orientation;
- participation and informed choice.

Walton (1985b), also of Harvard, developed the concept of mutuality:

> The new HRM model is composed of policies that promote mutuality – mutual goals, mutual influence, mutual respect, mutual rewards, mutual responsibility. The theory is that policies of mutuality will elicit commitment which in turn will yield both better economic performance and greater human development.

And Foulkes (1986) underlined the strategic nature of HRM: 'Effective human resources management does not exist in a vacuum but must be related to the overall strategy of the organization.'

Since these pioneering statements were made the following main tenets of human resource management have emerged.

Employees as valued assets

The fundamental belief underpinning HRM is that sustainable competitive advantage is achieved through people. They should therefore be regarded not as variable costs but as valued assets in which to invest, thus adding to their inherent value.

Strategy and culture are important

Organizational effectiveness can significantly be increased by paying close attention to the development of integrated business and human resource strategies, and by shaping the culture of the organization. A longer-term perspective in managing people and in developing an appropriate corporate culture is seen as important. Every aspect of employee management must be integrated with business management and must reinforce the desired company culture.

Emphasis on commitment rather than on compliance

The optimum utilization of human resources will be achieved by developing consistent and coherent policies which promote commitment to the organization, and unleash the latent creativity and energies of the people who work there, thus leading to enhanced performance. Fowler (1987) has suggested that one of the main themes of HRM is that 'a dominant emphasis on the common interests of employer and employed in the success of the business will release a massive potential of initiative and commitment in the workforce'.

AIMS OF HRM

The aims of human resource management are derived directly from the philosophical statements given above. These aims can be summarized as follows:

- to enable management to achieve organizational objectives through its workforce;
- to utilize people to their full capacity and potential;
- to foster commitment from individuals to the success of the company through a quality orientation in their performance and that of the whole organization (Guest 1987);
- to integrate human resource policies with business plans and reinforce an appropriate culture or, as necessary, reshape an inappropriate culture;

- to develop a coherent set of personnel and employment policies which jointly reinforce the organization's strategies for matching resources to business needs and improving performance;
- to establish an environment in which the latent creativity and energy of employees will be unleashed;
- to create conditions in which innovation, teamworking and total quality can flourish;
- to encourage willingness to operate flexibly in the interests of the 'adaptive organization' and the pursuit of excellence.

THE ROOTS OF HRM

The phrase 'human resource management' is not new. It was used as long as 40 years ago, but at that time it was interchangeable with personnel management (some people would claim that it still is). The philosophy of HRM, as described in this chapter, did not emerge in its complete form until the mid 1980s, but its roots go back to the 1960s and it was influenced by further developments in thinking about people and organizations in the 1970s and early 1980s.

The pioneers

The roots of HRM go back to the pioneering work of Drucker (1955) and McGregor in the 1960s. Drucker (1955) virtually invented management by objectives (although he never actually used that phrase). He wrote that: 'An effective management must direct the vision and effort of all managers towards a common goal'. This concept of visionary, goal-directed leadership is fundamental to HRM. He castigated personnel managers for their obsession with techniques that become gimmicks, and for their inability to get really involved in the business. And he referred to personnel management as 'a collection of individual techniques without much internal cohesion – a hodge podge'.

The emphasis in the HRM approach on coherence and internal consistency followed the Drucker line. He also stressed that human resources should be regarded as an organizational asset, thus expressing what later became the basic philosophy of HRM.

McGregor (1960) advocated management by integration and self-control as a strategy for managing people which affects the whole business. A key role of the personnel function, as he saw it, was to 'devise means of getting management to examine its assumptions, to consider the consequences and to compare it with others'.

Like Drucker, McGregor therefore paved the way to the basic HRM concept that human resource plans must be integrated with those of the business.

The behavioural science movement

The behavioural science movement came into prominence in the 1960s.

Its leading members were as follows.

- Maslow (1954), whose hierarchy of human needs placed self-actualization at the top of the pyramid.
- Likert (1966), who developed his integrating principle of supporting relationships. This stated that organization members should, in the light of their values and expectations, view their work as supportive, and as contributing to the building and maintenance of their sense of personal worth and importance.
- Argyris (1957), who believed that organization design should plan for integration and involvement, and that individuals should feel that they have a high degree of self-control over setting their own goals and over the paths defining those goals.
- Herzberg (1957), who advocated job enrichment as a means of improving organizational effectiveness.

The behavioural science movement had a somewhat idealistic flavour about it, but it did make two useful contributions to HRM. First, it underlined the importance of integration and involvement and, secondly, it highlighted the idea that management should accept as a basic value the need to increase the quality of working life as a means of obtaining better motivation and improved results.

The organization development movement

The organization development (OD) movement of the 1960s and 1970s was closely associated with the concepts of the behavioural scientists. The OD approach concentrates on overall organizational effectiveness, especially with regard to 'process' – how people behave in situations where they are constantly interacting with one another. Team development and the management of change were often important features of an OD programme. Particular attention was paid to the analysis of group processes and OD consultants evolved methods of analyzing organizational behaviour, especially within and between groups, and of solving conflict problems.

In particular, Schein (1969) developed methodologies for process consulting. This involves helping clients to generate information which they can understand about their projects and problems, and creating conditions for them to own the solutions to their problems by gaining internal commitment to their choice.

These concepts and approaches were linked to the views of the corporate culture analysts and have been incorporated in both the philosophy and methodology of HRM.

The corporate culture analysts

The corporate culture analysts such as Pascale and Athos (1981) and

Peters and Waterman (1982) suggested a number of attributes of successful companies which have strongly influenced HRM thinking about the need for strong cultures and commitment.

Pascale and Athos emphasized the importance of 'superordinate goals' – the significant meanings of the guiding concepts (ie values) with which an organization imbues its members.

Peters and Waterman suggested that the following attributes characterize the 'excellent companies'.

- *Productivity through people* – they really believe that the basis for productivity and quality is the workforce. They do not pay lip-service to the slogan 'people are our most important asset'. Instead, they do something about it by encouraging commitment and getting everyone involved.
- *Hands-on, value-driven* – the people who run the organization get close to those who work for them and ensure that the organization's values are understood and acted upon.
- *Visionary leadership* – the value-shaping leader is concerned with 'soaring lofting visions that will generate excitement and enthusiasm. Clarifying the value system and breathing life into it are the greatest contributions a leader can make'.

WHY HRM?

Against this background, why did HRM emerge as the dominant philosophy for managing people in the 1980s?

Perhaps the most important reason is that chief executives, prompted by economic and business trends, and the views of a number of influential writers such as those mentioned above and Kanter (1984), at last began to appreciate that competitive advantage is achieved through their employees – ie that it is people who implement the corporate plan, and that they must do something about seeing that it happens in their own organization.

Porter (1985), another highly influential writer, encapsulated this view when he wrote: 'HRM is an integral part of the value chain at firm level'.

More detailed analyses of the reasons for HRM were given initially by American writers, especially the Harvard School, and these were followed by comments from British academics and managers.

The American analysis

The Harvard School provided a basic answer to the question 'Why HRM?', when they first formulated their concept of human resource management. The leading members of this school (Beer, Spector, Lawrence, Quinn Mills and Walton 1984) suggested that: 'Today many pressures are demanding a broader, more comprehensive and more strategic perspective with regard to the organization's human resources.' They listed the following pressures in the US:

- increasing international competition;
- increasing complexity and size of organizations;
- the technological revolution which 'makes novel patterns of organization viable and perhaps mandatory. A new window of opportunity is thus opened' (Pava 1985);
- slower growth and declining markets affecting the ability of organizations to offer advancement opportunities to high-potential employees;
- increasing education of the workforce causing corporations to re-examine their assumptions about the capacity of employees to contribute and therefore the amount of responsibility they can be given;
- changing values of the workforce which expects to be offered more scope to be involved in company affairs;
- more concern with careers and life satisfaction among employees;
- changes in workforce demographics forcing employers to re-examine their employment and development policies.

The UK answer

In the UK, the HRM philosophies developed in America were imported more or less intact in the mid 1980s, although a number of people have questioned the extent to which the assumptions of HRM are relevant in the UK (see Chapter 2).

The acceptance of HRM in the UK and elsewhere has been accelerated by the messages on the significance of corporate culture and the need to manage change delivered by American gurus such as those mentioned above. Their prescriptions for success in managing people (quick fixes in a complex world) have had an immediate appeal.

As a result there has been a marked shift in the language of management and, as Guest (1989b) wrote: 'HRM is an attractive option to managements driven by market pressures to seek improved quality, greater flexibility and constant innovation.'

The impact of global competition, complexity, technological change and shifts in employee values have affected UK as well as US chief executives, and it has been said by Fowler (1987) that 'HRM represents the discovery of personnel management by chief executives'. For years, chairmen in their annual reports have been paying lip-service to the message 'people are important'. Now, however, competitive pressures from one-culture, high-commitment firms, and changes in employees' expectations have indicated the need for action instead of words to obtain fuller use of their human resources. And as Purcell (1989) suggests: 'in the entrepreneurial 1980s HRM philosophy was aligned closely with prevailing ideas of enterprise and the freeing up of management initiatives'.

A further factor contributing to the development of HRM was the extended use of micro-processing technology. This has made individual jobs more self-contained, more skilled and more varied. The 1980s saw the emergence of the 'knowledge worker'. Traditional methods of dealing with shop floor and office workers are no longer appropriate.

Within organizations, increased decentralization and devolution of authority have highlighted the fact that line managers have total responsibility for all their resources. They can no longer rely on, for example, industrial relations specialists to bail them out if they get into difficulty with trade unions. This increase in managerial accountability means that they are forced to concentrate on getting added value from their staff. It has therefore created opportunities for them to become more involved in promoting distinct HRM philosophies and approaches.

This concern for maximizing the utilization of their human resources, and the trend towards flatter and more flexible organizations, multi-skilling and autonomous working groups in cellular manufacturing systems, has brought managers into more immediate contact with knowledge workers at all levels and more highly skilled operatives working individually or in teams. The need to maintain close contact has led many managements to change the old practice of only communicating with their workforces through their trade unions. An HRM approach to industrial relations has therefore been developed which involves bypassing the unions and appealing directly to employees. This distinctive HRM philosophy emphasizes the contribution of individuals and is not so concerned with employees collectively.

Hendry and Pettigrew (1990) summed up the outcome of these developments well when they suggested that as a movement, HRM expressed a mission to achieve a turnaround in industry: 'HRM was thus in a real sense heavily normative from the outset: it provided a diagnosis and proposed solutions.' They also suggested that: 'What HRM did at this point was to provide a label to wrap around some of the observable changes, while providing a focus for challenging deficiencies – in attitudes, scope, coherence, and direction – of existing personnel management.'

CONCLUSIONS

Human resource management is essentially a business-oriented philosophy concerning the management of people in order to obtain added value from them and thus achieve competitive advantage. It is a philosophy that appeals to managements who are striving to beat off increasing international competition and appreciate that to do this they must invest in human resources as well as new technology.

It has been said, however, that HRM is a 'catch-all phrase, reflecting general intentions but devoid of specific meaning' (Guest 1989b). It can indeed be described conceptually, as in this chapter, in which a normative view of HRM is taken which reflects a shift in emphasis from definitions of how the management of people *is* done to implicit expectations as to how it *should* be done. But this normative approach is in danger of becoming a basis for management rhetoric which may express good intentions, but contains no more than a set of assumptions and beliefs which are only meaningful if they can be shown to work in practice. The remaining parts of this book will consider the practical applications of each aspect of HRM, but before exploring the practicalities, it is necessary to consider the characteristic features and approaches of the normative version of HRM, and to review the reservations which have been expressed about the HRM concept.

Chapter 2

Features of HRM

There are a number of features which can be said to characterize an HRM approach and these are described below. But it should be noted that these characteristics of HRM will be applied in many distinctive ways in different organizations. HRM as practised in America, Japan, Britain or anywhere else will have features which will be affected by the economic and political environment, and the industrial relations climates and practices of the country. HRM will be approached quite differently by organizations within these countries, depending on their culture and tradition, on whether or not they are part of a multinational organization, and on their structure, technologies, products and markets.

When considering these characteristic features it is also necessary to develop a set of propositions to test how they are being or might be applied. Organizations must also take account of a number of important reservations about HRM before considering the extent to which they develop an HRM culture.

CHARACTERISTIC FEATURES

The most characteristic features of HRM are that:

- it is a top-management driven activity;
- the performance and delivery of HRM is a line management responsibility;
- it emphasizes the need for strategic fit – the integration of business and personnel strategies;
- it involves the adoption of a comprehensive and coherent approach to employment policies and practices;
- importance is attached to strong cultures and values;
- it places emphasis on the attitudinal and behavioural characteristics of employees;
- employee relations are unitarist rather than pluralist, individual rather than collective, high trust rather than low trust;
- organizing principles are organic and decentralized with flexible roles and more emphasis on teamwork;

- rewards are differentiated according to performance, competence or skill.

Top-management driven

HRM is management and business oriented. It is an approach to managing people which is governed by top management's aims for competitive advantage, added value from the full utilization of resources and, ultimately, improved bottom-line performance. Top management sets the direction and requires everyone to be fully committed to the pursuit of organizational goals. But HRM-minded chief executives will appreciate that they are responsible for 'articulating the agenda for change', managing the change process, and reinforcing or reshaping the culture of the organization, so that it is conducive to the realization of their vision of the future.

Performance and delivery of HRM

The performance and delivery of HRM is a management responsibility, shared among line (operational) managers and those responsible for running service or staff functions. Managers are wholly accountable for making the best use of their resources. As Legge (1989) has written:

> HRM is vested in line management as business managers responsible for coordinating and directing *all* resources in the business unit in pursuit of bottom-line results ... a clear relationship is drawn between the achievement of these results and the line's appropriate and proactive use of the human resources in the business unit.

There is a distinction between this approach and the established dogma that line managers, as managers of people, are personnel managers in the sense that they are responsible for implementing personnel policies provided for them by the personnel department.

This view implies that line managers 'do as they are told' when managing people. HRM states that they do what they believe to be appropriate within the context of top management's HRM policy guidelines. These guidelines may, however, be developed with the advice of the personnel department, which may also be charged with the responsibility for monitoring (but not directing) their application.

In many ways, this emphasis on the responsibility of top management and line managers for HRM as a process of managing a valued resource strategically is the most distinctive feature of human resource management.

Strategic fit

Guest (1989a) has suggested that the distinctive feature of HRM is not just

just the capacity to think strategically, but also the ability to take a specific view of the strategic direction which should be pursued. He stresses the need for strategic integration or fit which:

> Refers to the ability of the organization to integrate HRM issues into its strategic plans to ensure that the various aspects of HRM cohere, and for line managers to incorporate an HRM perspective into their decision making.

The concept of strategic fit emphasizes that:

> Personnel policies are not passively integrated with business strategy, in the sense of flowing from it, but are an integral part of strategy in the sense that they underlie and facilitate the pursuit of a desired strategy.
>
> Legge (1989)

And as Beer and Spector (1985) put it:

> Any HRM system should be integrated to attract and hold the right mix of people. It must also establish a working relationship among those people that will carry out the organization's strategic plan, once that plan has taken into account all relevant human resource constraints and opportunities. In other words, HRM policies need to fit the business strategy.

Coherence

It has been stated by Hendry and Pettigrew (1990) that: 'Minimal to our specification for HRM is coherence of personnel practices one with another, and their adaptedness to the corporation's strategy.'

HRM aims to provide an internally coherent approach with mutually reinforcing initiatives which avoids the piecemeal implementation of unrelated personnel practices (including the latest 'flavour of the month'). It minimizes the danger of treating personnel practices as isolated tasks which, as indicated by Beer and Spector (1985), 'get farmed out to specialists whose concerns are limited to avoiding obvious problems and ensuring technical consistency and accuracy within their particular areas of practice'.

Strong cultures and values

The importance attached to strong cultures and values is a central feature of HRM. It was as long ago as 1938 when Barnard said that 'the task of leadership is essentially one of shaping values'.

Strong cultures and values are espoused in HRM because they create commitment and mutuality. As Beer and Spector (1985) state:

> The values held by top management must, in fact, be considered a key factor in determining whether or not HRM policies and practices

can and will be unified.... The degree to which respect for individual employees infuses HRM practices is especially crucial. Employees will not continue to be emotionally involved in the affairs of the business if their contributions are not respected by their managers. Similarly, employees cannot be expected to be actively committed to the organization if the organization does not show its commitment to them.

HRM policies and practices in the fields of resourcing, training, development, performance management, reward, communications and participation can be used to express senior management's preferred organizational values, and can shape the culture of the organization by providing various 'levers for change'. By striving to make these policies and practices integrated and internally consistent, it is hoped that the HRM aims of increasing commitment and mutuality will be achieved.

Attitudinal and behavioural characteristics of employees

It has been suggested by Townley (1989) that HRM can be characterized by an increasing emphasis on the attitudinal and behavioural characteristics of employees. A company adopting an HRM philosophy will aim to recruit and develop employees who will fit in well with the culture of the organization, and whose attitudes and behaviour will support the achievement of corporate objectives. This could be described as the 'hearts and minds' approach or 'behavioural control', and the emphasis, again, is on using selection, training and communication processes to increase commitment.

Employee relations

HRM values, as was pointed out by Guest (1989b), are 'unitarist to the extent that they assume no underlying and inevitable differences of interest between management and workers ... and individualistic in that they emphasize the individual–organization linkage in preference to operating through group and representative systems'.

Those who support the more idealistic versions of HRM believe in the creation of trust between management and employees by policies which demonstrate 'respect for the individual' by adopting open, participative and democratic styles of management, and by stressing that employees, as well as shareholders, customers and suppliers, are stakeholders in the organization.

Organizing principles

We have seen that HRM evolved in response to environmental pressures which have forced organizations to be more competitive, responsive, flexible and adaptive to change. Organization structures have therefore had to respond to the particular needs and features of the business within its changing environment. This has involved more decentralization, so that operations are closer to the markets they serve. It has also involved giving managers more autonomy as well as more accountability for the results they achieve through the effective use of resources. Within organizations, roles in management teams and autonomous work groups have become more flexible and rely on people applying a wider range of skills (multi-skilling).

The reward system

The reward system can be used as a lever for change to develop a more performance-oriented culture and to encourage the acquisition of new skills. Rewards can be differentiated according to performance (performance-related pay) and competency or skill-based pay structures can be evolved. The reward system is operated more flexibly and is linked to a performance management scheme.

APPROACHES TO HRM

The features described above may characterize a stereotyped HRM system, but the extent to which HRM is applied, and *how* it is applied, will vary considerably according to the type of organization and the environment in which it operates. As discussed in this section, the approach will be governed by the policy goals of the enterprise and may be hard or soft depending on the philosophy of top management. But it is possible to devise a model of the HRM cycle which describes broadly how it operates.

Policy goals

Guest (1989b) has commented that HRM provides 'a coherent and distinctive set of propositions about an approach to management ... which seeks to make the best use of the most recent research to promote positive organizational outcomes'. He suggests that this approach should be based on four policy goals.

1 *Strategic integration* – ensuring that human resource and business strategies are integrated, coherent HRM policies and practices are evolved and that these are used by line managers as part of their everyday work.

2 *Commitment* – binding employees to the organization.

3 *Flexibility* – creating structures which are adaptive and receptive to innovation, basing job design on job enrichment or autonomous work

group principles and multi-skilling to meet the requirements of this type of design.

4 *Quality* – ensuring high-quality management and staff who deliver high-quality goods and services.

These policy goals, however, can be developed and applied in different ways and, as described below, there is more than one version of HRM.

Hard and soft HRM

A distinction has been made by Storey (1987) between hard and soft versions of HRM.

The 'hard' version emphasizes the 'quantitative, calculative and business strategic aspects of managing the head count resource in as "natural" a way as for any other economic factor'. Thus, employees are treated as just another part of the input–output equation. Hard HRM strategies are concerned with improving employee utilization (the cost-effective approach) and getting them to accept that their interests coincide with those of the organization (the unitarist approach). Resourcing strategies and practices will aim to recruit and develop employees who 'fit' the organization's culture. A hard HRM industrial relations strategy will develop direct links with individuals and groups of workers, and may bypass the trade unions and their representatives. In its extreme version, hard HRM will deliberately aim to marginalize trade unions (or do without them altogether). Employees will be involved in the improvement of quality and productivity, but are unlikely to participate in business decision making. This 'hard' version therefore stresses the *management* aspect of HRM.

The 'soft' version emphasizes communication, motivation and leadership. It is concerned with developing what Handy (1989) calls a 'culture of consent' and recognizes that employees cannot be treated just like any of the other resources because, unlike them, people feel and react. There is more emphasis on strategies for gaining commitment by informing employees about the company's mission, values, plans and trading conditions, involving them in how work should be organized, and grouping them in self-managing teams. A pluralist view is taken which recognizes that the needs of employees will not always coincide with those of the organization, and care is taken to balance the respective needs, so far as this is possible. If there are unions, it is recognized that they have a part to play in representing the collective interests of employees, but the company maintains its right to communicate directly to individuals.

A model of the HRM cycle

Whatever the extent to which an enterprise inclines towards either the hard or the soft version of HRM, the approach adopted attempts to be internally coherent. This can be represented by the model of the human resource management cycle developed by Tichy, Fombrun and Devanna (1982) shown in Figure 2.1.

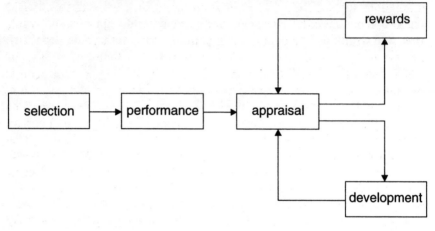

Figure 2.1 *The human resource cycle*

The four generic processes in this model which take place in all organizations are selection, appraisal, rewards and development.

These human resource elements are designed to impact on performance at both the individual and organizational levels. The model therefore indicates that performance is the key variable which HRM processes are intended to affect. This is achieved by selecting people who are best able to perform the jobs defined by the structure, appraising their performance, motivating them with appropriate rewards and developing them for the future. Performance is also a function of the organizational context and the resources surrounding the individual. Hence the importance of the organization's climate (working atmosphere), structure and systems, all of which impact on performance because of their influence on the ways in which people are organized and managed.

RESERVATIONS ABOUT HRM

Although HRM became very fashionable during the 1980s and many personnel directors were transmogrified into human resource directors (albeit with no discernible change in their roles), reservations have been expressed about just how 'real' HRM is. Commentators such as Armstrong (1987) have asked if HRM is simply a case of the emperor's new clothes (nothing really there at all) or of old wine in new bottles. In other words, is it just personnel management under another name, with an extra gloss of suspect entrepreneurial philosophy, 1980s style?

The issue of the differences, if any, between HRM and personnel management is discussed in Chapter 3. Writers like Guest (1991) may accept that there is such a thing as a distinctive HRM approach with a number of specific policy goals, but he refers to the 'optimistic but ambiguous label of human resource management', believes that 'HRM has been considerably talked up', and has expressed the view that while there is plenty of 'hope and hype' about HRM there is little real achievement. He suggests that evidence from the US (Guest 1990) and the UK (Marginson 1989, Storey and Sisson 1989) reveals considerable diversity of practice, raising doubts about the extent of its application.

The fact that HRM is not being applied universally does not destroy its philosophical base or its aspirations. The strongly-held beliefs that human resources should be treated as valued assets and that people should be developed to become more 'resourceful humans' are valid. Their advocacy of a strategic and coherent approach is equally worth while. And their aspirations for increasing commitment and use of human resources to the full are also valid – from management's point of view.

However, other reservations have been expressed about the morality of HRM, its practicality, its approach to industrial relations, and the contradictions inherent in the pursuit of strong cultures and flexibility, and in the focus on individualism and teamwork.

Morality of HRM

In spite of all their protestations to the contrary, the advocates of HRM could be seen to be introducing alternative and more insidious forms of control by emphasizing the need for employees to be committed to what the organization wants them to do. As Legge (1989) pointed out:

> In its emphasis on 'strong culture', in theory HRM is able to achieve a cohesive workforce, but without the attendant dilemma of creating potentially dysfunctional solidarity. For a 'strong culture' is aimed at uniting employees through a shared set of managerially sanctioned values ('quality', 'service', 'innovation' etc) that assume an identification of employee and employer interests. Such co-optation – through cultural management of course – reinforces the intention that autonomy will be exercised 'responsibly', ie in management's interests.

In other words, say the accusers, HRM is manipulative. They note that chief executives with a mission for HRM tend to adapt the principle of 'what is good for General Motors is good for America' to that of 'what is good for the business must be good for everyone in it'. Such executives could be right, but not always, and the forces of internal persuasion and propaganda may have to be deployed to get people to accept values with which they may not be in accord and which, in any case, may be against their interests.

HRM implies some form of 'behavioural control' and as Wickham (1976) wrote:

> If control in work organizations is through 'technical rules' it is hardly a problem should the worker possess a distinct cultural identity. As control is through the worker's 'normative orientations', the necessary control in work will depend on the removal of any basic cultural differences between him and his superiors.

This accusation of manipulation is probably the most difficult for HRM enthusiasts to refute. The favoured answer is 'Yes, we are seeking the commitment of everyone to the organization's objectives and values, but those individuals *will* receive benefits in the shape of opportunities for promotion and development, rewards and security if the organization prospers. Surely, therefore, if the values are worthwhile ones such as quality and customer service, it is proper for us to ask everyone to support them.' This assertion can only be justified if the organization tries its hardest to share its success with those who have contributed to it, truly believes in its professed values and acts upon them.

Practicality

To put HRM into practice – which involves strategic integration, developing a coherent and consistent set of employment policies, and gaining commitment – requires high levels of determination and competence at all levels of management, and a strong and effective personnel function staffed by business-oriented people. It is difficult to meet these criteria, especially when the proposed HRM culture conflicts with traditional managerial attitudes and behaviour.

The development of integrated HR strategies, a central feature of HRM, is difficult if not impossible in companies which lack any real sense of strategic direction. Business strategies, where they are formulated, tend to be dominated by marketing considerations, leading to product and systems developments. To support these, priority is given, understandably enough, to obtaining financial resources and maintaining a sound financial base. Human resource considerations often come off a poor second.

The creation of coherent HRM policies may also be more difficult to apply in divisionalized companies or conglomerates where authority is devolved to strategic business units. The corporate office may be solely concerned with exercising financial control, leaving the units to get on with whatever approach to personnel management they believe will be most profitable. The latter may adopt an HRM approach, but this is less likely without strong leadership from the top.

Moreover, is the HRM prescription too simplistic? As Fowler (1987) wrote of the HRM message to top management:

This tends to be beguilingly simple. Don't bother too much about the techniques or content of personnel management. Just manage the context. Get out from behind your desk, bypass the hierarchy, and go and talk to people. That way you will unlock an enormous potential for improved performance.

There is nothing fundamentally wrong with that prescription, but there is more to HRM than culture management and direct communications. Commitment needs to be matched to competence. HRM is also about developing people and enabling them to make the best use of their abilities in their own interests, as well as those of the organization. And this means the creation and deployment of a range of integrated personnel policies and techniques, and the education and training of line managers in the key part they play in implementing them.

HRM and the trade unions

As Fowler (1987) has suggested:

At the heart of the concept (of HRM) is the complete identification of employees with the aims and values of the business–employee involvement but on the company's terms. Power, in an HRM system, remains very firmly in the hands of the employer. Is it really possible to claim full mutuality when at the end of the day the employer can decide unilaterally to close the company or sell it to someone else?

American writers like Walton (1985a) contrast the 'control strategy' (adversarial labour relations, emphasis on interest conflict) with the 'commitment strategy' (mutuality in labour relations, joint planning and problem solving in expanded agendas; unions, management and workers redefine their respective roles). And Beer and his Harvard colleagues (1984) state that 'the competitive pressure from one-culture, high-commitment firms is the primary stimulus for questioning traditional adversarial systems'.

This American concept of industrial relations in an HRM environment does not fit in well with the British, indeed European, tradition of the role of trade unions. In Britain, since the Donovan Commission (1968), a pluralistic approach that recognizes the distinct interests of the employer and trade union members has been the backcloth of a voluntary system which is reinforced by local collective bargaining arrangements. Although Conservative legislation has reduced the power of trade unions by, for example, outlawing the closed shop, they are still a powerful force with a valuable role to play. Their place and contribution in an HRM system has to be accepted wherever trade unions are recognized or where it is appropriate for them to be recognized.

Strong cultures and flexibility

HRM stresses the need for both strong cultures and flexibility. But a powerful, all-pervading culture could inhibit flexibility by requiring people to conform to certain values and norms. Even if flexibility is a stated value it may be difficult to act upon it if all the other pressures are forcing people into a mould of the company's making.

It can be argued, however, that strong cultures do allow a rapid response to familiar conditions because the dominant ideology guides people in the action to be taken. But they can 'still inhibit immediate flexibility in response to the unfamiliar, because of the commitment generated to a (now) inappropriate ideology' (Legge 1989).

The only answer to this problem is to bear in mind that one of the main strategic choices available to organizations is that of innovation. This must, therefore, be one of the key values, which has to be supported by stressing the need for flexibility and by the creation of mutually dependent task forces and work groups whose brief would be to work flexibly in the pursuit of innovative goals.

Individualism and teamwork

The emphasis on strong cultures in HRM aims not only to give direction, but also, in Legge's (1989) words, 'to mediate the tension between individualism and collectivism, as individuals socialised into a strong culture are subject to unobtrusive collective controls on attitudes and behaviour'. The attempt to mediate this tension can lead to internal inconsistencies in HRM practice. These are created as companies develop individual, performance-related reward systems, and extol the virtue of individual competence and ambition, while at the same time advocating better teamwork and setting up autonomous working groups whose success depends on the members of the group working well and flexibly together.

Organizations have to rely upon a combination of individual endeavour and teamwork to achieve success. In developing and applying HRM philosophies and policies, both these considerations have therefore to be borne in mind. But it is not easy, and this raises another question mark about the practicality of HRM in its fullest sense.

The problem with commitment

The concept of commitment is beguiling, but the question has to be asked 'Commitment to what?'. The organization requires commitment to its own values, but individuals have other loyalties and values which affect their behaviour – to their family, their trade union, their profession or craft, or their personal integrity.

The meaning of commitment is also unclear, and the extent to which it can be developed and the impact of higher levels of commitment on performance (if they can be achieved), are matters for debate. This issue is discussed in Chapter 8.

CONCLUSIONS

A powerful HRM philosophy has been developed with a number of characteristic features. As summed up by Purcell (1989), in HRM:

> The human resource management function becomes recognized as a central business concern; its performance and delivery are integrated into line management; the aim shifts from merely securing compliance to the more ambitious one of winning commitment. The employee resource therefore becomes worth investing in, and training and development thus assume a higher profile.

These features, plus the value placed on strategic integration and coherence, add up to a distinctive approach to managing people. But it is not an easy option. It is difficult to apply in practice and there are a number of internal inconsistencies to be resolved. Finally, there is the important question of how HRM fits in with personnel management and vice versa, which is addressed in the next chapter.

Chapter 3

HRM and Personnel Management

INTRODUCTION

Many people feel that HRM offers nothing new and is just a meaningless (and transatlantic) label which has been attached to personnel management. Effective personnel managers have always practised HRM, and when they are informed of this fact they might well echo Molière's *Bourgeois Gentilhomme* when he exclaimed 'Good heavens! For more than 40 years I have been speaking prose without knowing it.'

This view that 'it's all the same really' was summed up by Lowry (1990) when he pointed out that:

> Personnel work has always included strategic matters and the present emphasis on business issues merely represents another change in the environment to which the personnel manager adapts by strengthening the competences needed for the new situation. Human resource management is just the continuing process of personnel management – it is not different.

This is a convincing argument, but it could be said that awareness among personnel managers of the need to be more strategically and business oriented might not have developed to its present state without the influence of the HRM concept.

This chapter considers the relationship between HRM and personnel management under the following headings:

- the similarities between HRM and personnel management;
- the differences between HRM and personnel management;
- the role of the personnel function in an HRM culture.

SIMILARITIES

The similarities between personnel management and HRM are as follows.

1   Personnel management strategies, like HRM strategies, flow from the business strategy.

2 Personnel management, like HRM, recognizes that line managers are responsible for managing people. The personnel function provides the necessary advice and support services to enable managers to carry out their responsibilities.

3 The values of personnel management and at least the 'soft' version of HRM are identical with regard to 'respect for the individual', balancing organizational and individual needs, and developing people to achieve their maximum level of competence, both for their own satisfaction and to facilitate the achievement of organizational objectives.

4 Both personnel management and HRM recognize that one of their most essential processes is that of placing the right people in the right jobs, thus ensuring that the organization's human resources are matched to ever-changing organizational requirements.

5 The same range of selection, appraisal, training, management development and reward management techniques are used in HRM and in personnel management.

6 Personnel management, like the 'soft' version of HRM, attaches importance to the processes of communication and participation within an employee relations system.

DIFFERENCES

The differences between personnel management and human resource management can be seen as a matter of emphasis and approach rather than one of substance. Or, as Hendry and Pettigrew (1990) put it, HRM can be perceived as a 'perspective on personnel management and not personnel management itself'.

The contrasts made by Pettigrew and Whipp (1991) as set out in Table 3.1 are mainly concerned with management style and organization rather than with differences in technique.

Another formulation of the differences between personnel management and HRM (Table 3.2) has been produced by Storey (1992) on the basis of a study by the Warwick University Industrial Relations Research Unit. Again, the emphasis is on beliefs, assumptions and process rather than techniques.

Table 3.1 *Personnel management and human resource management – an outline*

Element	Personnel management	Human resource management
Employee relations	Adversarial	Developmental and collaborative
Orientation	Reactive and piecemeal	Proactive and business focused
Organization	Separate functions	Integrated functions
Client	Management	Management and employees
Values	Order, equity consistency	Client and problem focused, tailored solutions
Role of specialist	Regulatory and record keeping	Problem sensing, tailored solutions
Role of line management	Passive ownership	Active ownership
Overall output	Compartmentalized thinking and acting	Linking various human resource levers to business needs

(Reproduced with permission from A M Pettigrew and R Whipp 1991, *Managing Change for Competitive Success*, Oxford, Blackwell)

Table 3.2 *Differences between personnel and industrial relations and HRM*

Dimension	Personnel and IR	HRM
Beliefs and assumptions		
Contract	Careful delineation of written contracts	Aim to go 'beyond contract'
Rules	Importance of devising clear rules/mutuality	'Can do' outlook; impatience with 'rule'
Guide to management action	Procedures/consistency control	'Business need'/flexibility/ commitment
Behaviour referent	Norms/custom and practice	Values/mission
Managerial task vis-a-vis labour	Monitoring	Nurturing
Nature of relations	Pluralist	Unitarist
Conflict	Institutionalized	De-emphasized
Standardization	High (eg 'parity' an issue)	Low (eg 'parity' not seen as relevant)
Strategic aspects		
Key relations	Labour-management	Business-customer
Initiatives	Piecemeal	Integrated
Corporate plan	Marginal to	Central to
Speed of decision	Slow	Fast
Line management		
Management role	Transactional	Transformational leadership
Key managers	Personnel/IR specialists	General/business/line managers
Prized management skills	Negotiation	Facilitation
Key levers		
Foci of attention for interventions	Personnel procedures	Wide-ranging cultural, structural and personnel strategies
Selection	Separate, marginal task	Integrated, key task
Pay	Job evaluation; multiple, fixed grades	Performance-related; few if any grades
Conditions	Separately negotiated	Harmonization
Labour-management	Collective bargaining contracts	Towards individual contracts
Thrust of relations with stewards	Regularized through facilities and training	Marginalized (with exception of some bargaining for change models)
Communication	Restricted flow/indirect	Increased flow/direct
Job design	Division of labour	Teamwork
Conflict handling	Reach temporary truces	Manage climate and culture
Training and development	Controlled access to courses	Learning companies

(Reproduced with permission from J Storey 'HRM in action: the truth is out at last.' *Personnel Management*, April 1992.)

From her review of the literature, Legge (1989) has identified three features which seem to distinguish HRM and personnel management.

1   Personnel management is an activity aimed primarily at non-managers, whereas HRM is less clearly focused, but is certainly more concerned with managerial staff.

2   HRM is much more of an integrated line management activity, whereas personnel management seeks to influence line management.

3   HRM emphasizes the importance of senior management being involved in the management of culture, whereas personnel management has always been rather suspicious of organization development and related unitarist, social-psychologically orientated ideas.

The strategic nature of HRM is another difference commented on by a number of people who, in effect, dismiss the idea that traditional personnel management was ever really involved in the strategic areas of business. Hendry and Pettigrew (1990), for example, believe that the strategic character of HRM is distinctive.

Perhaps the most significant difference is that HRM is based on a management and business-oriented philosophy. It is a central, senior management-driven strategic activity, and it is developed, owned and delivered by management as a whole to promote the interests of the organization which they serve.

Hence the importance attached to strategic integration and strong cultures, which flow from top management's vision and leadership, and which require people who will be committed to the strategy, will be adaptable to change, and will fit the culture. By implication, as Guest (1991) says, 'HRM is too important to be left to personnel managers'. So what is the role of personnel managers in an HRM culture?

ROLE OF PERSONNEL MANAGERS IN AN HRM CULTURE

Limitations of traditional personnel management

Commentators on the growth and acceptance of a distinctive HRM approach have sometimes suggested that this was because traditional personnel management had failed to rise to the occasion – the need to innovate and to rethink the organization's approach to managing people.

For example, Beer and Spector (1985) concluded that existing personnel practice is:

All too frequently a hodge-podge of policies based on little more than outmoded habits, current fads, patched-up responses to former crises and pet ideas of specialists. HRM practice urgently needs to be reformed from the perspective of general management. HRM issues are much too important to be left largely to specialists.

Guest (1991) commented that:

Personnel departments typically operate a complex system of controls, justified in part by legislative requirements, in part by the need for manpower control/systems at the centre. This is likely to encourage a focus on administrative efficiency and associated problem-solving. It implies little capacity for or interest in innovation, except possibly in systems improvements. This bureaucratic, administrative and sometimes policing role helps to explain why one image of personnel management among some line managers is of a 'bureaucratic nuisance'.

Tyson and Fell (1986) believe that:

Classical personnel management has not been granted a position in decision-making circles because it has frequently not earned one. It has not been concerned with the totality of the organization but often with issues which have not only been parochial but esoteric to boot.

And Legge (1989) suggested that:

In Britain, 'personnel management' evokes images of do-gooding specialists trying to constrain line managers, of weakly kowtowing to militant unions, of both lacking power and possessing too much power. Our new enterprise culture demands a different language, one that asserts management's right to manipulate, *and* ability to generate and develop resources.

A further reason for the limited impact made by some personnel managers is the perception that they are the people in the middle, mediating between management and employees. Thomason (1976), for example, sees personnel management as increasingly assuming a third-party role between management and employee, especially with the development of legislation. And Mackay and Torrington (1986) stated:

Personnel management is never identified with management interests, as it becomes ineffective when not able to understand and articulate the aspirations of the workforce.

It is indeed a valid role for personnel managers to act as the conscience of management when balancing the needs of the organization and of its employees. It is also necessary for them to be able to contribute to the development of personnel policies on the basis of an understanding of the expectations and values of employees. But positioning themselves too firmly in the middle could leave them in a limbo, without any capacity for influencing human resource strategies and practices to the benefit of both the organization and its employees.

What personnel managers can contribute

Essentially, as Legge (1978) has suggested, personnel managers can contribute 'unique non-substitutable expertise'. Torrington (1989) goes as far as stating that:

> The recruitment, development and management of resourceful humans is a more complex, interesting and expert task than the management of human resources.

He believes that:

> Personnel management remains a distinctive management specialism whose practitioners derive their expertise from an understanding of the ways in which people, individually and collectively, engage with the need to be employed and the needs of organizations to employ them.

No one could disagree with the latter statement, but it could be argued that the development and management of resourceful humans is just as much the responsibility of line managers as that of personnel specialists, perhaps even more so.

However, in an HRM culture, expertise in the technicalities of personnel management, although important, is not enough. Personnel managers have to be innovators as well as technicians. Legge (1978) has identified two alternative methods by which personnel managers seek to exert influence in organizations. The *conformist innovator* is the personnel specialist who identifies with organizational success, emphasizing cost benefit and conforming to the criteria adopted by managerial colleagues, who usually have greater power. In contrast, the *deviant innovator* identifies with a set of norms which are distinct from, but not necessarily in conflict with, the norms of organizational success. Power drives from an independent, professional stance for working with managerial clients. As Torrington (1989) comments:

> conformist personnel management innovators do no more than reflect the competences and values of their colleagues. Deviant personnel innovators are able to make a distinctive contribution to the totality of management, which becomes richer and more powerful as a result.

HRM AS AN OPPORTUNITY, NOT A THREAT

Some personnel specialists see HRM as a threat:

> *They* (meaning line managers) are going to take away from *us* (meaning personnel managers) our reasons for existence, except as administrators of personnel systems.

Others, including this writer, see HRM as an opportunity to use one's expertise both in furthering the objectives of the business and in meeting the needs, expectations and values of those who work in it. The management-driven nature of HRM means that line managers should be more receptive to the creative interventions 'deviant innovators' can make.

HRM provides the opportunity for personnel directors to be more involved because they can play an equal part in making business decisions; feeding into the debate human resource considerations and thus contributing to the formulation of business strategy. By being involved at this stage they are in a much better position to develop personnel strategies which flow from the business strategy, to institute coherent 'people programmes' (resourcing, training and development, reward and employee relations) which directly support the achievement of strategic goals, to provide for the full utilization of individual abilities and to ensure that a proper balance is maintained between organizational and individual needs.

Personnel managers in an HRM culture can be enablers, ensuring that management is able to exercise its responsibility for human resources effectively. Enabling takes place through creative interventions, and involves the provision of guidance and support. As Peter Hobbs, Group Personnel Director of The Wellcome Foundation, has said of personnel specialists (Armstrong 1989a):

> We are enablers. We may often present managers with some of the stars in the firmament and say 'Hey, isn't that nice?' and get people to reach for them. But we are enabling other people to do things rather than doing things ourselves.

Personnel managers in an HRM context are also 'architects' in the Tyson and Fell (1986) typology, who ensure that explicit personnel policies exist as part of the corporate strategy. They take a long-term view, and human resource planning and development are important activities. Systems tend to be sophisticated. The head of the personnel function is probably on the board and his or her power is derived from professionalism and perceived contribution to the business.

But this is a demanding requirement. The HRM model requires personnel managers to avoid, in Guest's (1989a) words, the 'piecemeal introduction of techniques without the strategic integration to ensure their impact'. And as Armstrong (1989b) expressed it:

> Personnel directors who remain in their corner nursing their knowledge of the behavioural sciences, industrial relations tactics and personnel techniques, while other directors get on with running the business, cannot make a fully effective contribution to achieving the company's goals for growth, competitive gain and the improvement of bottom-line performance. It is not enough for personnel

directors just to understand the business and its strategy: their role must be built into the fabric of the business.

LEVERS FOR CHANGE

The development of HRM within an organization requires changes – to attitudes, behaviour, processes, systems and structures. Personnel specialists working with line management can make a major contribution to creating and maintaining an HRM system because of the powerful levers for change available to them. These levers comprise:

- *HRM strategy* – formulating strategies which set clear directions for long-term development and provide the basis for building a coherent approach to personnel management;
- *organization* – helping with the restructuring of organizations and the redesign of jobs to fit projected changes in product or systems development, technologies, decentralization and ownership;
- *culture management* – influencing behaviour and, thereby, attitudes through resourcing, performance management, development and reward strategies, and helping to get the mission and values of the organization defined, understood, accepted and acted upon;
- *change management* – using knowledge of the factors which influence commitment to change, and devising programmes and methods of introducing change accordingly;
- *managing commitment* – introducing communication, participation and performance systems, and implementing educational programmes designed to increase identification with the company's mission and values, and develop behaviour and attitudes which support their achievement;
- *flexibility* – developing and implementing flexibility strategies to make the best use of human resources and enable people to learn and apply a wider range of skills;
- *teamworking* – enhancing the ability of people to work well together and making the best use of the synergies resulting from effective teamwork and of the increased motivation achieved by being part of an autonomous work group;
- *quality management* – assisting with the introduction of total quality management approaches through education and training processes, and involving people in quality improvement programmes;
- *resourcing* – matching human resources to the changing requirements of the organization;
- *human resource development* – investing in the training and development of all levels of the workforce, and relating those training programmes to the needs of the organization and individuals to improve performance and extend their knowledge base;

- *performance management* – introducing systems which clarify objectives at all levels in the organization and measure performance against those objectives, in order to agree improvement and development plans;
- *reward management* – using the reward management system to define performance expectations to reward people according to their contribution;
- *employee relations* – developing a cooperative climate of employee relations which allows direct communication to employees but, where appropriate, recognizes the role unions play in a pluralist organization.

The rest of this book explores ways in which these levers for change can be applied in an HRM setting.

Part II

HRM at Corporate Level

Chapter 4

Strategic HRM

THE BASIS OF STRATEGIC HRM

A strategic orientation is a vital ingredient in human resource management. It provides the framework within which a coherent approach can be developed to the creation and installation of HRM policies, systems and practices.

Definition

Strategic human resource management is concerned with those decisions which have a major and long-term effect on the employment and development of people in the organization, and on the relationships which exist between its management and staff.

An HR strategy will express the intentions of the enterprise about how it should manage its human resources. These intentions provide the basis for plans, developments and programmes for managing change.

Aim

The aim of strategic human resource management is to ensure that the culture, style and structure of the organization, and the quality, commitment and motivation of its employees, contribute fully to the achievement of business objectives.

Relationship to business strategies

HR strategies flow from and support the achievement of business strategies. But they are not reactive. They can play a proactive role by helping to form business strategies through culture management and by providing a framework of reference relating to human resources for those who create the business strategy. This input spells out how the organization can maximize the added value provided by its human resources. It can identify the human resource strengths and weaknesses of the enterprise so that business strategies are formulated which take into account how the strengths can be utilized and developed, and the weaknesses overcome.

Human resource considerations at the business strategy formulation stage mainly refer to broad organizational issues relating to changes in structure and culture, company performance, matching resources to future requirements and the approach that should be taken to the achievement of commitment to strategic change (change management will be discussed in Chapter 7).

Support to the implementation of business strategies is provided by studying their HR implications and deciding what directions should be taken to help achieve them. These can take the form of resourcing, development, reward, employee relations, motivation or commitment strategies.

Thus, those responsible for HR strategy help to shape business strategies and also ensure that 'strategic fit' is obtained between those strategies and those relating to the human resource. This means, as Legge (1989) puts it:

> Personnel policies are not passively integrated with business strategy in the sense of flowing from it but are an integral part of the strategy in the sense that they underlie and facilitate the pursuit of a desired strategy.

Main features of strategic human resource management

It has been suggested by Hendry and Pettigrew (1986) that the main features of strategic human resource management are as follows:

■   the use of planning;
■   a coherent approach to the design and management of personnel systems based on an employment policy and manpower strategy, often underpinned by a philosophy;
■   HRM activities and policies are matched to some explicit business strategy;
■   the people of the organization are seen as a strategic resource for achieving competitive advantage.

This chapter takes a holistic view of HR strategy as an integrating force and discusses how this can be achieved. To do this it is necessary to:

■   examine briefly what business strategy is, how it is developed and the forms it takes;
■   assess how HR strategy can be integrated with the business strategy;
■   consider the components of HR strategy and approaches to its development.

BUSINESS STRATEGY

Definition

Business strategy determines the direction in which the enterprise is going in relation to its environment in order to achieve sustainable competitive advantage. Strategy is a declaration of intent which is concerned with the long-term allocation of significant company resources. It is the means of addressing critical issues or success factors at the level of the business as a whole or an aspect of it – for example, a business unit or function. Strategic decisions aim to make a major and long-term impact on the behaviour of the organization.

Features of business strategy

Business strategy, as Miller (1983) points out, is a market-led concept affected by product–market considerations and directed at the achievement of competitive advantage. The tendency is for management to react to its environment rather than to anticipate it. The logic of the competitive environment dictates action.

Business strategy is not monolithic; neither are there any general rules as to how it should be developed or expressed. Within the same organization there will be different levels of strategy, and the approach to strategy formulation in diversified companies will vary.

Levels of business strategy

There are two levels of business strategy. At the corporate level the strategy is likely to be concerned in general with the composition and performance of the overall portfolio of the businesses which make up the company. In particular, corporate strategy refers to:

- the cohesiveness of that portfolio;
- mergers, acquisitions and divestments;
- the company's mission;
- the ethos on how to manage and control the business.

At the business unit level, strategies are mainly concerned with answering the question 'Where and how are we going to compete and earn sustained high returns?'. This means making decisions on how, in the longer term, the business can develop superior effectiveness, a superior cost position and superior quality, coupled with the ability to meet customers' real needs.

Corporate strategies are put into effect at the competitive level by business strategies which refer to:

- definition of the business;

- growth and profitability objectives;
- product/market scope;
- marketing approach;
- competitive position.

These business unit considerations are also the ones most likely to concern medium-sized or smaller independent companies which, however, are less likely to have an articulated business strategy.

Strategic direction

There are three broad directions in which business strategies can go. First, they can be innovation led, which may result in the development of sophisticated HRM policies designed to gain commitment to strategic change and to enable the organization to adapt rapidly to new circumstances. The emphasis will be on making full use of human resources by investing in training and development, and by introducing more effective methods of motivation.

Secondly, they may be principally concerned with maintaining market share rather than increasing it. In this case, HR strategies will concentrate on achieving organizational stability.

A third direction for business strategies is to be cost led, in which case HR strategies will be aimed at achieving the efficient use of labour and the emphasis will be on cost-effectiveness.

Approaches to strategy in diversified companies

On the basis of their research into how the corporate offices of 16 British-owned diversified companies managed their relationships with their business units, Goold and Campbell (1986) discussed how the centre tackles its roles of setting and reviewing strategies, resource allocation, planning reviews, and controlling and auditing performance. They refer to Lawrence and Lorsch's (1976) views that superior performance in diversified companies depends upon the ability of each business unit to attune its objectives, strategies and culture to its competitive environment. The problem is achieving a balance between the business unit strategies, which are tailored to their own circumstances, and the role of the centre in providing policies and a structure which integrates the divisions into a corporate whole.

Goold and Campbell identified three styles of managing strategy which address how this balance is achieved by means of different corporate approaches to influencing business unit strategies. These are as follows.

1   *Strategic planning companies*, which believe that they should partici-
    pate in and influence the development of business unit strategies by
    establishing demanding planning processes and making contributions

of substance to strategic thinking. They are at their best in helping businesses to embark on strategies to build long-term competitive advantage. They encourage a wide search for the best strategies, are willing to coordinate between businesses if needed, and provide a buffer against capital market pressures. They believe the best approach to defining strategy and motivating management is cooperative and collaborative, with an emphasis on shared purposes. Companies with this style included BOC, BP, Cadbury Schweppes, Lex, STC and UB.

2 *Strategic control companies*, which are concerned with business unit planning, but believe in organizing around independent profit-responsible business units, and leaving as much as possible of the initiative to business unit management. The centre therefore focuses more on establishing demanding planning processes, and on reviewing and criticising business unit proposals, than on advocating particular strategies. Tight control is exercised against results achieved, taking into account both financial and strategic objectives. Companies with this style included Courtaulds, ICI, Imperial Group, Plessey and Vickers.

3 *Financial control companies*, where the centre sees its main tasks as sanctioning expenditure, agreeing targets, monitoring performance against the targets and taking action to reorganize management teams which are performing poorly. They have no formal planning systems and are concerned mainly with financial results which they control against annual targets. This contrasts with strategic control companies which try to measure strategic achievements and take a longer-term view of performance against targets. Companies with this style included BTR, Hanson Trust, GEC, Tarmac and Ferranti.

Goold and Campbell conclude that the strategic management style adopted by the centre with regard to its business units should be shaped by the nature of the unit's business and the resources available to the corporation as a whole.

Development of business strategy

The analysis of the concept of business strategy as a basis for HR strategy has to take account not only of the different levels and styles of strategy, but also of the diversity of ways in which strategy is formed. It is generally assumed that this is an analytical, systematic and rigorous process. But this is not necessarily so. As Johnson (1987) comments:

Strategic decisions are characterized by the political hurly-burly of organizational life with a high incidence of bargaining and a trading-off of costs and benefits of one interest group against another; all within a notable lack of clarity in terms of environmental interests and objectives.

Goold and Campbell also emphasize the variety and ambiguity of influences which shape strategy:

> Informed understandings work alongside more formal processes and analyses. The headquarters agenda becomes entwined with the business unit agenda, and both are interpreted in the light of personal interests. The sequence of events from decision to action can often be reversed, so that 'decisions' get made retrospectively to justify actions that have already taken place.

Strategy formulation is not necessarily a rational and continuous process, as was pointed out by Mintzberg (1987). He believes that, rather than being consciously and systematically developed, strategy reorientations happen in what he calls brief 'quantum loops'.

Strategies, according to Mintzberg, are not always deliberate. In theory, he says, strategy is a systematic process. 'First we think, then we act. We formulate then we implement.' In practice, 'a realized strategy can emerge in response to an evolving situation' and the strategic planner is often 'a pattern organizer, a learner if you like, who manages a process in which strategies, and visions, can emerge as well as be deliberately conceived'.

Strategic management is therefore not the logical and linear approach which dominated management thinking in the late 1960s and the 1970s. The formulation of strategy is usually an evolutionary and incremental process. And as Pettigrew and Whipp (1991) point out:

> Business strategy, far from being a straightforward, rational phenomenon, is in fact interpreted by managers according to their own frame of reference, their particular motivations and information.

Articulating business strategies

Because of the factors mentioned above, business strategies are not necessarily expressed in writing, although there are advantages in doing so from the point of view of having a defined point of reference for planning and control purposes. Strategic management and strategic control companies are more likely to prepare formal, long-term strategic plans, but financial control companies will rely entirely on one-year budgets with interim reforecasts as required.

A business unit or independent company may have a formal strategy but it is more likely, especially in the latter case, to have an unwritten strategic orientation which is based on an assessment of future market opportunities. In Mintzberg's phrase, these organizations 'craft' their strategies, being responsive to changing situations as they emerge, while still taking a view on the general direction in which they are going.

INTEGRATING BUSINESS AND HUMAN RESOURCE STRATEGY

Strategic integration is necessary to provide congruence between business and human resource strategy so that the latter supports the accomplishment of the former and, indeed, helps to define it. The aim is to provide strategic fit and consistency between the policy goals of human resource management and those of the business.

This point was originally made by Fombrun, Tichy and Devanna (1984) who stated that:

> Just as firms will be faced with inefficiencies when they try to implement new strategies with outmoded structures, so they will also face problems of implementation when they attempt to effect new strategies with inappropriate HR systems. The critical management task is to align the formal structure and the HR systems so that they drive the strategic objectives of the organization.

Guest (1989b) has suggested that strategic human resource management is largely about integration. Its concern is to ensure that HRM:

> is fully integrated into strategic planning so that HRM policies cohere both across policy areas and across hierarchies and HRM practices are used by line managers as part of their everyday work.

Miller (1989) emphasizes that the key to effective HR strategy is 'the concept of "fit": the fit of human resource management with the thrust of the organization'.

Problems of integration

This is easier said than done for the following reasons.

1   *Diversity of strategic processes, levels and styles* – as described above, the different levels at which strategy is formulated and the different styles adopted by organizations may make it difficult to develop a coherent view of what sort of HR strategies will fit the overall strategies and what type of HR contributions are required during the process of formulation.

It has been argued by Miller (1983) that to achieve competitive advantage, each business unit in a diversified corporation should tailor its HRM policy to its own product–market conditions, irrespective of the HRM policies being pursued elsewhere in the corporation. If this is the case, there may be coherence within a unit, but not across the whole organization, and it may be difficult to focus HR strategies on corporate needs.

But in a financial control type of corporation there may be no pressure for the creation of a corporate culture and HR strategies to support it. In such cases, HR strategy is formed at unit level and the only time a serious problem is likely to emerge is if units have to be merged.

2 *The evolutionary nature of business strategy* – this phenomenon, and the incremental nature of strategy making, may make it difficult to pin down the HR issues which are likely to be relevant. As Hendry and Pettigrew (1990) suggest, there are limits to the extent to which rational HR strategies can be drawn up if the process of business strategic planning is itself irrational.

3 *The absence of written business strategies*, which adds to the problems of clarifying the business strategic issues which human resource strategies should address.

4 *The qualitative nature of HR issues* – business strategies tend, or at least aim, to be expressed in the common currency of figures and hard data on portfolio management, growth, competitive position, market share, profitability etc. HR strategies may deal with quantifiable issues such as resourcing and skill acquisition but are equally likely to refer to qualitative factors such as commitment, motivation, good employee relations and high employment standards. And Purcell (1989) has written:

> If it were possible to demonstrate that enlightened or progressive approaches to the management of people were invariably associated with higher productivity, lower unit costs and improved profit, life would be easier for the human resource planner. As it is, little can be proved because of the complexity of the variables and the impossibility of monitoring and measuring all the relevant dynamics and relationships.

Approaches to dealing with these problems

These are serious problems and it may be difficult for the HR strategist to overcome them completely. But the attempt should be made and the following approaches are available.

Understand how business strategies are formed

The HR strategist should take pains to understand the levels at which business strategies are formed and the style adopted by the company in creating strategies and monitoring their implementation. It will then be easier to focus on those corporate or business unit issues which are likely to have HR implications.

Understand the key business issues

The key business issues which may impact on HR strategies include:

- intentions concerning growth or retrenchment, acquisitions, mergers, divestments, diversification, product–market development;
- proposals on increasing competitive advantage through productivity, improved quality/customer service, cost reduction;
- the felt need to develop a more positive, performance-oriented culture;
- any other culture management imperatives associated with changes in the philosophies of the organization in such areas as moving from control to commitment, mutuality, communications, involvement, devolution and teamworking.

Business strategies in these areas should not be over-influenced by HR factors. HR strategies are, after all, about making business strategies work. But the business strategy must take into account key HR opportunities and constraints.

Business strategy sets the agenda for HR strategy in the following areas:

- resourcing;
- skills acquisition and development;
- culture, values and attitudes;
- commitment;
- productivity;
- performance management;
- rewards;
- employee relations.

While these may all arise at the business unit level there are a number of decisive issues which exist at the corporate level. These are:

- mission;
- values, culture and style;
- organizational philosophy and approach to the management of people;
- top management as a corporate resource.

Some organizations such as IBM, Hewlett-Packard and Marks and Spencer will have clearly articulated strategies in these areas. Others will not, until events enforce a re-evaluation of the mission, values, philosophies and structure of the organization, as has happened recently in such companies as British Airways, BP, Thorn EMI and ICL. These changes have often taken place following the appointment of a new chief executive officer with a powerful vision of the direction the organization should take.

Establish methods of linking business and HR strategies

Business and HR issues influence each other and in turn influence corporate and business unit strategies. It should be remembered, however, that in establishing these links, account must be taken of the fact that strategies for change have also to be integrated with changes in the external and internal environments (strategic change issues will be discussed in Chapter 7).

As suggested by Cooke and Armstrong (1990), to achieve a link in rigorous terms requires a means of quantifying the additional resources allocated to HR overall, and at the level of each element of HR strategy, and measuring and comparing the marginal return on investing in each element. But this approach is unlikely to be practicable.

The link must therefore be judgemental, but it can still be rigorous. Conceptually, the approach would be to develop a matrix, as illustrated in Table 4.1, which for each of the key elements of business strategy identifies the associated key elements of HR strategy.

Table 4.1 *A conceptual approach to linking business and HR strategies*

	Market development	**Product development**	**New technology**	**Other**
Organization				
Resourcing				
Training				
Performance management				
IR				
Other				

DEVELOPING HUMAN RESOURCE STRATEGIES

Human resource strategy contributes to the business strategy but is also justified by it. The aim should be to make it imaginative, innovative, clear and actionable. It must also be selective, focusing on priorities, and flexible, rapidly adjusting to change. HR strategy should be formulated by a continuous process of analyzing what is happening to the business and where it is going. The related business and human resource questions are set out in Table 4.2.

Table 4.2 *Strategic questions*

Business	Human resource
1 What business are we in and what is our mission?	What sort of people do we need in the business to achieve our mission?
2 Is our present culture value system appropriate?	How can any changes required to our culture and value system be achieved?
3 Where are we going?	What are the implications of these plans on the future structure, HR systems and resource requirements?
4 What are our strengths, weaknesses, opportunities and threats?	To what extent are these strengths and weaknesses related to our human resource capability? What opportunities have we got to develop and motivate our staff? What are the threats in the shape of skills shortages, the retention of key staff, productivity, motivation and commitment? And what are we going to do about them?
5 What are the main strategic issues facing the business?	How do these issues affect the structure, systems and human resource requirements of the business?
6 What are the critical success factors which determine how well we achieve our mission?	How far will business success be helped or hindered by the quality, motivation, commitment and attitudes of our employees?

THE ROLE OF THE HR DIRECTOR

How do heads of the HR function get involved in strategic planning? The answer, of course, is that they should be in a position to do so by being members of the executive board or committee. In that capacity, they should be capable of taking a full part in a business discussion. As Cooke and Armstrong remark, 'They must not be relegated to a metaphorical corner and only come to life when there is a threatened strike or a shortage of systems analysts.'

HR directors need to be able to pose and suggest answers to such fundamental questions as the following.

- What is the nature of the corporate culture? Is it supportive or dysfunctional?
- What needs to be done to define or redefine our values in such areas as quality, customer service, innovation, teamworking and responsibility of the organization for its employees?
- What do we need to do to increase commitment? How do we communicate our intentions and achievements to employees and what steps do we take to obtain feedback from them, and to involve them in company affairs?
- What kind of skills do we need in the future?
- Are performance levels high enough to meet demands for increased profitability, higher productivity, better quality and improved customer service?
- Will the organization's structure and systems be able to cope with future challenges in their present form?
- Are we making the best use of the skills and capacities of our employees?
- Are we investing enough in developing those skills and capacities?
- Are there any potential constraints in the form of skills shortages or industrial relations problems?

The answers to these and similar questions define the areas in which HR strategies need to be developed. The important thing is to give an overall sense of purpose to HR activities by linking them explicitly to the needs of the business and its employees.

Chapter 5

HRM and Organization Management

WHAT IS INVOLVED?

Organizations are made up of individual people whose roles interact. They are best regarded as systems which exist within an ever-changing and often turbulent environment in order to transform inputs (human, financial or physical resources) into outputs (goods or services). This transformation is achieved by the use of technology, and operational and administrative systems, which take place by means of various processes within a structure and are influenced by the culture of the organization.

The structure, culture, processes and systems of an organization are interdependent. The common factor in all these aspects of organization is the human resource – the managers, professional and technical staff, knowledge workers, skilled workers, office workers and operatives whose efforts are combined to achieve the purpose of the organization.

Human resource management is a strategic approach to the motivation and development of people, and to gaining their commitment so that they can make their best contribution to organizational success, while also meeting their own needs and aspirations. HRM takes place within the context of the organization and must therefore be concerned with how it is structured, the use it makes of people and the impact of its processes and systems on this interaction, commitment and performance.

Organization management

Organization management is based on an understanding of how organizations function, and this is discussed in the next section of this chapter. It is then concerned with:

- structure (dealt with in this chapter);
- culture management (see Chapter 6);
- the processes of strategic management, operational management and leadership as discussed in this chapter, and of change management, achieving flexibility, teamworking and quality management as described in later chapters;

- the systems used in the organization; these comprise HR systems such as performance and reward management as described later in this book, and operational and administrative systems covering such things as management information, management accounting, production control and distribution.

HOW ORGANIZATIONS FUNCTION

Formal and informal structure

The structure of an organization consists of units and functions. These contain positions in which job holders are accountable for achieving results. Between these positions relationships exist which require the exercise of authority and the exchange of information. In the traditional 'command and control' structure there is, therefore, what used to be called a 'chain of command' which starts at the top and defines a hierarchy of positions, indicating who is accountable to whom for what.

A defined organization structure attempts to describe how the overall management task has been divided into a number of activities and to indicate how these activities are directed, coordinated and controlled. The structure may be presented in organization charts and manuals which set out the formal organization of relationships and describe who is supposed to do what.

The command and control structure as described above is, however, not a satisfactory model for the way in which today's organizations actually function. First, many organizations find they have to operate more flexibly and recognize that it is *collective* effort which achieves organizational ends. In this type of fluid, responsive and adaptive organization, authoritarianism no longer works. What has to be developed is a teamwork approach which involves devolving responsibility to largely autonomous work groups and recognizing that the organization has to develop a culture of consent.

Secondly, the formal organization, as so described, may usefully define the theoretical framework for getting things done, but it cannot convey *how* that work is done. There is, in fact, a powerful informal organization, as was first suggested by Barnard (1938). He believed that organizations are cooperative systems, not the products of mechanical engineering or of paperwork bureaucracies. He advocated natural groups within the organization, upward communication and leaders who function as cohesive forces. He emphasized the significance of the informal roles and relationships which strongly influence the way the formal structure operates.

Factors affecting structure

It was suggested by Chandler (1962) that 'structure follows strategy'. In other words, the structure must be designed to support the achievement of the company's strategic goals.

The business strategy will be developed in the light of an 'environmental scanning' process to analyze the impact of both external and internal environmental factors on the organization. The environment and the rate at which it changes will have a major effect on how organizations function.

As a result of their research, Burns and Stalker (1961) established that in stable conditions a highly structured or 'mechanistic' organization emerges with specialized functions, clearly defined roles, strict administrative routines and a hierarchical system of exercising authoritarian control. In effect, this is the bureaucratic system. However, when the environment is volatile, a rigid system of ranks and routines inhibits the organization's speed and sensitivity of response. In these circumstances the structure is, or should be, 'organic' in the sense that it is a function of the situation in which the enterprise finds itself, rather than conforming to any predetermined and rigid view of how it should operate. Individual responsibilities are less clear cut and members of the organization must relate constantly what they are doing to its general situation and to specific problems.

A contingency model of organization was developed by Lawrence and Lorsch (1967). Organization, as they define it, is the process of coordinating different activities to carry out planned transactions within the environment. The three aspects of environment upon which the design of the organization is contingent are the market, the technology (ie the tasks carried out), and research and development. These may be differentiated in relation to such dimensions as rate of change and uncertainty. This process of reacting to complexity and change by *differentiation* creates a demand for effective *integration* if the organization as a whole is to adapt efficiently to the environment.

New concepts of organization

Until fairly recently, organization theory and practice was dominated by certain 'principles of organization', referring to such matters as span of control and unitary command ('one man, one boss'). They were handed down on tablets of stone by the pioneering writers on management. These principles, as Burns and Stalker (1961) imply, may have been applicable in bureaucratic and mechanistic paper factory or mass production organizations, operating in relatively stable conditions. But they are no longer applicable as generalizations in today's more turbulent environment. Following the universal introduction of high-grade information technology, Drucker (1988) suggested that:

The typical large business 20 years hence will have fewer than half the levels of management of its counterpart today, and no more than a third the managers.... Businesses, especially large ones, have little choice but to become information-based. Demographics, for one, demands the shift. The centre of gravity in employment is moving fast from manual and clerical workers to knowledge workers who resist the command-and-control model that business took from the military 100 years ago.

Adhocracy

'Adhocracy' was the term given by Mintzberg (1981) to organizations which were highly innovative and had to be capable of responding quickly to rapid change. In adhocracies the structure is fluid, power is constantly shifting, and coordination and control are achieved through the informal communication and interaction of competent experts. 'With power based on expertise instead of authority, the line/staff distinction evaporates.' The main characteristics of adhocracies are the importance of expertise, fluid organization structures and the extensive use of project teams and task forces.

The federal organization

The devolvement of authority and decentralization so that managers work closer and more responsively to their markets is leading, according to Handy (1989), to the creation of a new type of federal organization. This takes the process of decentralization one stage further by establishing each key operational, manufacturing or service provision activity as a distinct, federated unit. Every federal entity runs its own affairs, although they are linked together by the overall strategy of the organization and, if it is a public company, are expected to make an appropriate contribution to corporate profitability in order to provide the required return on their shareholders' investments and to keep external predators at bay.

The centre in a federal organization maintains a low profile. The federated activities are expected to provide the required initiative, drive and energy. The centre is at the middle of things, not at the top. It is not just a banker but it does provide resources. Its main role is to coordinate, advise, influence, suggest and help to develop integrated corporate strategies.

New organization models – empiricism, flexibility and teamwork

Developments in organization theory and practice during the 1980s and early 1990s have been mainly empirical. The visible presence of 'new, flexible competitors', as Peters (1988) put it; the need to respond to change, challenge and uncertainty; and the impact of new technology, have all combined to emphasize the need for flexibility and teamwork.

The processes of federalizing and flattening organizations (stripping out layers of middle management) have added to this emphasis.

Kanter (1989) has described this as the 'post-entrepreneurial corporation'. This represents a triumph of process over structure:

> relationships and communication and the flexibility to temporarily combine resources are more important than the 'formal' channels and reporting relationships represented in an organizational chart.... What is important is not how responsibilities are divided but how people can pull together to pursue new opportunities.

Peters also suggests that new flexible manufacturing systems and the decentralized availability of the information needed for fast product changeover are leading to the wholesale adoption of cellular manufacturing, 'which eventually concentrates all the physical assets needed for making a product in a self-contained configuration which is tailor-made for team organization'. His prescription for the new model organization is:

- the creation of self-managing teams, responsible for their own support activities such as budgeting and planning;
- managers who act as 'on call' experts, spending most of their time helping teams;
- managers who encourage constant front-line contact among functions;
- no more than five layers of structure;
- the use of small units – 'small within big' configurations everywhere.

Organizations such as British Petroleum (BP) are replacing large, formal, hierarchical departments with small, flexible teams, many of them cross-functional, and some of them temporary. The emphasis is on 'networking', in which a broad group of people communicate openly and informally as the need arises. Each team does have a leader, but, in the words of a BP 'Project 1990' document: 'Managers are there to support and empower their staff, not to monitor or control their activities.' The BP head office organization chart has been dubbed 'The Egg' because the various functions such as finance, human resources, corporate strategy, research and IT (information technology) strategy are depicted as a number of elements which network together within an overall context (expressed in an oval shape), but are not linked by formal control and communication channels.

The emphasis on teamwork, networking and informality in the new organization extends, as in BP, to the top where there is an increasing tendency to adopt a 'collegiate' approach in which people share responsibility and are expected to work with their colleagues outside their primary function or skill.

AN HRM APPROACH TO ORGANIZATION DESIGN

HRM is concerned with giving people the scope and opportunity to use their skills and abilities to better effect. Jobs should be designed to satisfy the requirements of the organization for productivity, operational efficiency and quality of product or service. But they must also meet the needs of individuals for interest, challenge and accomplishment. These aims are interrelated and the aim of job design is to integrate the needs of the individual with those of the organization.

When it comes to designing or modifying the structure a pragmatic approach is necessary. First, ensure that you understand the environment, the technology and the existing systems of social relationships. Then design an organization which is *contingent* upon the circumstances of the particular case. There is always some choice, but designers should try to achieve the best fit they can. And, in making their choice, they should be aware of the structural, human and systems factors which will influence the design, and of the context within which the organization operates. They must also take into account the culture of the organization, the processes which take place in it and the effect all this has on relationships, on individuals and on groups within the organization. This empirical approach will be largely influenced by environmental and cultural factors (cultural factors will be discussed in Chapter 6), and it will have to take particular note of the needs for flexibility and good teamwork.

Organization design is ultimately a matter of ensuring that the structure and methods of operation fit the strategic requirements of the business and its technology within its environment. Disruption occurs if internal and external coherence and consistency is not achieved. And, as Mintzberg (1981) suggests:

> Organizations, like individuals, can avoid identity crises by deciding what they wish to be and then pursuing it with a healthy obsession.

ORGANIZATION PROCESSES

Organization design, however, is only one aspect of organizational management. Account has also to be taken of the processes of strategic management, operational management and leadership.

Strategic management

Strategic management is the process by which an organization formulates objectives and long-range plans and is managed so as to achieve them. Strategic goals may be grouped broadly under Porter's (1985) three headings: innovation, quality enhancement and cost reduction.

Strategic management requires:

- the determination of medium and long-term objectives – the strategic intent;
- the selection of a coherent strategy to achieve these objectives;

- the direction of the organization so that it moves constantly towards their achievement.

Strategic management is concerned with both ends and means. As an end, it describes a vision of what something will look like in a few years' time. As a means, it shows how it is expected that the vision will be realized. Strategic management is therefore visionary management, concerned with creating and conceptualizing ideas of where the organization should be going. But it is also empirical management, which decides how, in practice, it is going to get there.

The focus is on identifying the organization's mission and strategies, but attention is also given to the resource base required to make it succeed. It is always necessary to remember that strategy is the means to create value. Managers who think strategically have a broad and long-term view of where they are going. But they are also aware that they are responsible for improving bottom-line performance in the shorter term.

A strategy of quality enhancement might be encapsulated, as in Motorola Inc, into a drive for total customer satisfaction. This could be expressed as five major concerns:

1 Is *authority* allocated appropriately to respond and commit to the customers' expectations?

2 Is the *strategy* such that it will optimize market share and return on net assets while totally satisfying the customer?

3 Is the *structure* supportive of the strategy and sufficiently flexible to elicit the most creative and disciplined contributions from our associates?

4 Do we have the *systems* in place to facilitate high-quality, short-cycle time pursuit of our strategies?

5 Do we have *performance* expectations, enhancement tools and measurements which create the environment and skill sets to achieve total customer satisfaction?

The answers to these questions provided the basis for defining three key HRM issues.

1 Employees must understand the business issues in order actively to participate in the internal changes in response to external forces.

2 The company must have an infrastructure to facilitate global communication at all levels.

3 The company must work constantly towards a unity of purpose in its worldwide workforce, using every opportunity possible.

Operational management

Operational managers are there to get results which will further the achievement of the organization's strategic goals. In theory they apportion their time logically between planning, organizing, motivating and controlling activities. In practice, their activities are characterized by brevity, variety and fragmentation. Although they may be planning, organizing etc from time to time, these activities tend to get submerged in the hurly-burly of organizational life. As Mintzberg (1973) comments:

> The manager actually appears to prefer brevity and interruption to his work. He becomes conditioned by his workload; he develops an appreciation of the opportunity cost of his own time; and he lives continuously with an awareness of what else might or must be done at any time. Superficiality is an occupational hazard of the manager's job.... The manager gravitates to the more active elements of his work – the current, the well-defined, the non-routine activities.

These characteristics of the work of operational managers need to be borne in mind by HR specialists when they are advising on new HR systems such as performance management (see Chapter 13). If managers perceive these to be just an additional administrative chore they will not play their part in operating them properly. This will defeat the whole purpose of such a system which is that it is something for managers to use as part of their everyday life to help them to improve their own performance and that of their staff.

Leadership

Leaders have a key role to play in developing effective organizations. They set people in the right direction and motivate them to achieve goals by satisfying their needs, and by stressing the value of their contribution. They recognize and reward success, which not only gives people a sense of accomplishment, but also helps them to feel that they belong to an organization which cares for them.

As Kotter (1980) has written:

> The direction-setting aspect of leadership does not produce plans; it creates visions and strategies. These describe a business, technology or corporate culture in terms of what it should become over the long term and articulate a feasible way of achieving this goal.

Burns (1978) distinguishes between two types of leaders:

- *transactional,* who exchange money, jobs and security for compliance;
- *transformational,* who motivate others to strive for higher-order goals rather than merely short-term interest.

One might expect that it is transformational leaders who are most likely to turn their visions into reality, but there will be occasions when transactional leaders, who have a clear idea of what they want, will be able to achieve their goals by enlisting compliance rather than commitment.

There is no leadership style that guarantees success in all situations. Fiedler (1967) emphasized some time ago the 'situational' aspects of leadership:

> Leadership performance then depends as much on the organization as on the leader's own attributes. Except perhaps for the unusual case, it is simply not meaningful to speak of an effective leader and an ineffective leader; we can only speak of a leader who tends to be effective in one situation and ineffective in another.

There are, of course, charismatic leaders who sweep aside their followers' doubts and problems concerning their daily tasks by inspiring them with a vision of what is to be achieved. But effective leaders do not necessarily have to be charismatic. Non-charismatic leaders who rely on their know-how, their ability to give an impression of quiet confidence and their cool, analytical approach to solving problems can be equally, if not more, effective in some situations. Such leaders can be described as enablers and empowerers. They provide the right sort of guidance, they give people scope to act and they ensure that their staff have the skills and knowledge to achieve their tasks. They encourage their staff to participate and they spend a lot of time generating commitment to the achievement of objectives.

THE ROLE OF THE HR SPECIALIST IN ORGANIZATION MANAGEMENT

The management of organizations is, in effect, human resource management. It is, therefore, the prime responsibility of line managers. But HR specialists should be well qualified to provide advice on structures, processes and systems based on their understanding of the requirements of the organization in human resource terms and their knowledge of the factors to be taken into account in organization and job design. They can help to implement the visions of the charismatic leader through communication, education and training processes, and they have to play a major part in identifying what sort of people the new organization needs and how they are going to be obtained through recruitment or development. Where a transactional approach is being adopted by the chief executive, the HR specialist can advise on the type of performance management and reward systems which are most likely to deliver results.

Chapter 6

HRM and Culture Management

WHAT IS CULTURE MANAGEMENT?

Culture management is the process of developing or reinforcing an appropriate culture – that is, one which helps the organization to fulfil its purpose.

Culture management is concerned with the following.

- *Culture change*, the development of attitudes, beliefs and values which will be congruent with the organization's mission, strategies, environment and technologies. The aim is to achieve significant changes in organizational climate, management style and behaviour, which positively support the achievement of the organization's objectives.
- *Culture reinforcement*, which aims to preserve and reinforce what is good or functional about the present culture.
- *Change management*, which is concerned with enabling the culture to adapt successfully to change and gaining acceptance to changes in organization, systems, procedures and methods of work (see Chapter 7).
- *Commitment gain*, which is concerned with the commitment of members of the organization to its mission, strategies and values (see Chapter 8).

Aims of culture management

The aims of culture management are to:

- develop an ideology which guides management on the formulation and implementation of coherent HRM strategies and policies;
- create and maintain a positive climate within an organization that indicates the behaviour which is expected of members of that organization in the course of their work;
- promote understanding and commitment to the values of the organization.

Culture management does not, however, aim to impose a uniform and bland culture on an organization. It recognizes that different cultures may be appropriate in different parts of the firm. And, although there will be certain values which management believe are important, the process of disseminating these values will recognize that members of the organization will have their own sets of values which they will only modify if they are convinced that it is in their own interests, as well as those of the organization.

The management of the organization's culture is a central activity for senior management with the advice and help of HR specialists in their increasingly important role as internal consultants (this role is discussed in the last section of this chapter).

Managements, according to Legge (1989), use strong culture to unite employees through a set of managerially sanctioned values. They set the direction and establish a culture which helps them to maintain it. Legge also points out that:

> The relationship between 'strong' cultures, employee commitment and adaptability contains a series of paradoxes. Strong cultures allow for a rapid response to familiar conditions, but inhibit immediate flexibility in response to the unfamiliar because of the commitment generated to a (now) inappropriate ideology.

Weak cultures are potentially more adaptable, but will not be so effective in generating commitment to action.

The implication is that the pursuit of new strategic goals in response to environmental changes may require action to change the culture. However, changing strong cultures can be a prolonged affair, except in crisis conditions.

Culture management as a process should be based on an understanding of the significance and scope of corporate culture as discussed below.

SIGNIFICANCE AND SCOPE OF CORPORATE CULTURE

Definition

Corporate culture is the pattern of shared beliefs, attitudes, assumptions and values in an organization which may not have been articulated, but in the absence of direct instructions, shape the way people act and interact, and strongly influence the ways in which things get done.

This definition emphasizes that corporate culture refers to a number of abstractions (beliefs, attitudes etc) which pervade the organization, although they may not have been defined in specific terms. Nevertheless, they can influence people's behaviour significantly.

A more comprehensive psychologist's definition was provided by Schein (1984):

Organizational culture is the pattern of basic assumptions that a given group has invented, discovered or developed in learning to cope with its problems of external adaptation and internal integration, and that have worked well enough to be considered valid, and, therefore, to be taught to new members as the correct way to perceive, think and feel in relation to those problems.

The importance of culture to organizations

Corporate culture is a key component in the achievement of an organization's mission and strategies, the improvement of organizational effectiveness and the management of change.

The significance of culture arises because it is rooted in deeply-held beliefs. It reflects what has worked in the past, being composed of responses which have been accepted because they have met with success.

Corporate culture can work for an organization by creating an environment which is conducive to performance improvement and the management of change. It can work against an organization by erecting barriers which prevent the attainment of corporate strategies. These barriers include resistance to change and lack of commitment.

The impact of culture can include:

- conveying a sense of identity and unity of purpose to members of the organization;
- facilitating the generation of commitment and 'mutuality';
- shaping behaviour by providing guidance on what is expected.

Corporate culture can be described in terms of *values, norms and artefacts*. It will be perceived by members of the company as *organizational climate*, and it will influence, and be influenced by, the organization's strategy, structure and systems.

Values

Values refer to what is regarded as important. They are expressed in beliefs on what is best or good for the organization and on what sort of behaviour is desirable. The 'value set' of an organization may only be recognized at top level, or it may be shared throughout the firm so that the enterprise could be described as being 'value driven'.

Clearly, the more strongly based the values the more they will affect behaviour. This does not depend upon their having been articulated. Implicit values, which are deeply embedded in the culture of an organization and are reinforced by the behaviour of management, can be highly influential, while espoused values which are idealistic and are not reflected in managerial behaviour may have little or no effect.

Value areas in which values can be expressed might be:

- care and consideration for people;
- care for customers;
- competitiveness;
- enterprise;
- equity in the treatment of employees;
- excellence;
- growth;
- innovation;
- market/customer orientation;
- priority given to organizational rather than to people needs;
- performance orientation;
- productivity;
- provision of equal opportunity for employees;
- quality;
- social responsibility;
- teamwork.

Values are translated into reality through *norms* and *artefacts* as described below. They may also be expressed through the media of language (organizational jargon), rituals, stories and myths.

Norms

Norms are the unwritten rules of behaviour, the 'rules of the game' which provide informal guidelines on how to behave. Norms tell people what they are supposed to be doing, saying, believing, even wearing. They are never expressed in writing – if they were, they would be policies or procedures. They are passed on by word of mouth or behaviour and can be enforced by the reactions of people if they are violated. They can exert very powerful pressure on behaviour because of these reactions – we control others by the way we react to them.

Norms refer to such aspects of behaviour as the following.

- How managers treat subordinates and how subordinates relate to their subordinates.
- The prevailing work ethic, eg 'Work hard, play hard', 'Come in early, stay late', 'If you cannot finish your work during business hours you are obviously inefficient', 'Look busy at all times', 'Look relaxed at all times'.
- Status – how much importance is attached to it; the existence or lack of obvious status symbols.
- Ambitions – naked ambition is expected and approved of, or a more subtle approach is the norm.
- Performance – exacting performance standards are general; the highest praise that can be given in the organization is to be referred to as very professional.

- Power – recognized as a way of life; executed by political means; dependent on expertise and ability rather than position; concentrated at the top; shared at different levels in different parts of the organization.
- Politics – rife throughout the organization and treated as normal behaviour; not accepted as overt behaviour.
- Loyalty – expected, a cradle to grave approach to careers; discounted, the emphasis is on results and contribution in the short term.
- Anger – openly expressed; hidden, but expressed through other, possibly political, means.
- Approachability – managers are expected to be approachable and visible; everything happens behind closed doors.
- Formality – a cool, formal approach is the norm; first names are/are not used at all levels; there are unwritten but clearly understood rules about dress.

Artefacts

Artefacts are the visible and tangible aspects of an organization which people hear, see or feel. Artefacts can include such things as the working environment, the tone and language used in letters or memorandums, the manner in which people address each other at meetings or over the telephone, and the welcome (or lack of welcome) given to visitors and the way in which telephonists deal with outside calls. Artefacts can be very revealing.

Organizational climate

Organizational climate is less encompassing than the concept of organizational culture and is more readily measured.

Organizational climate is how people perceive (see and feel about) the culture that has been created in their company or unit. It has been defined by French, Kast and Rosenzweig (1985) as 'the relatively persistent set of perceptions held by organization members concerning the characteristics and quality of organizational culture'.

Perceptions about climate can be measured by questionnaires such as that developed by Litwin and Stringer (1968), which cover nine categories.

1   *Structure* – feelings about constraints and freedom to act, and the degree of formality or informality in the working atmosphere.

2   *Responsibility* – the feeling of being trusted to carry out important work.

3   *Risk* – the sense of riskiness and challenge in the job and in the organization; the relative emphasis on taking calculated risks or playing it safe.

5 *Warmth* – the existence of friendly and informal social groups.

6 *Support* – the perceived helpfulness of managers and co-workers; the emphasis (or lack of emphasis) on mutual support.

7 *Standards* – the perceived importance of implicit and explicit goals and performance standards; the emphasis on doing a good job; the challenge represented in personal and team goals.

8 *Conflict* – the feeling that managers and other workers want to hear different opinions; the emphasis on getting problems out into the open rather than smoothing them over or ignoring them.

9 *Identity* – the feeling that you belong to a company; that you are a valuable member of a working team.

Management style

Management style describes the way in which managers set about achieving results through people. It is how managers behave as team leaders and how they exercise authority. Managers can tend to be autocratic or democratic, tough or soft, demanding or easy-going, directive or *laissez-faire*, distant or accessible, destructive or supportive, task oriented or people oriented, rigid or flexible, considerate or unfeeling, friendly or cold, keyed up or relaxed. How they behave will depend partly on themselves – their natural inclinations, partly on the example given to them by their managers and partly on organizational values and norms.

Culture and strategy

To paraphrase Chandler (1962), it seems possible that culture follows strategy; in other words, strategic choices on such matters as growth, innovation, product–market development and human resource development will shape behaviour and, progressively, change values and norms. But the culture of the organization could equally help to shape its strategy. For example, a company with an open, enterprising and flexible culture is more likely to adopt this approach when developing its business strategies. Culture and strategy are interdependent.

Culture and process

Process is broadly 'the way things are done around here'. It embraces such aspects of organizational behaviour as leading, motivating, gaining commitment, managing change, working in teams, and planning and coordinating activities. Policies, procedures, structures and systems are means of making process work.

Culture management will involve influencing behaviour, attitudes and beliefs through process. For example, total quality as a concept can be developed through various quality control mechanisms, but will only be fully achieved if processes in the organization fully support its achievement.

Culture and structures or systems

Corporate culture will affect the ways in which the organization is structured and its operational systems. These will include the amount of rigidity or flexibility allowed in the structure, the extent to which informal processes of interaction and communication override or replace formal channels, the amount of authority which is devolved from the top or the centre, and the degree to which jobs are compartmentalized and rigidly defined. It may affect the number of layers of management, the spans of control of managers and the extent to which decisions are made by teams rather than by individuals.

The development and use of systems will also be affected by the corporate culture and will in turn help to shape it. A bureaucratic or mechanistic organization will attempt to govern everything through systems or manuals. An organic approach will only allow systems which are functions of the situation in which the enterprise finds itself, rather than conforming to any predetermined and rigid view of how it should operate. In some organizations, people follow systems to the letter, in others, people take pride in 'bucking the system' and cutting corners to get things done. Systems can be used as control mechanisms to enforce conformity or they can be flexed to allow scope for adapting and responding to new situations as they arise.

Evolution of culture

The norms and values which are the basis of culture will be evolved over time as a result of the influence of the organization's external environment and its internal processes, systems and technology.

The external environment covers economic, market, competitive and social trends, technological innovations and government interventions. Internally, culture is shaped by the purpose, strategy and technology of the organization and by particularly significant events, such as a major crisis or the impact of a dynamic, visionary and inspirational chief executive. In fact, the philosophy and values of top management over the years will have played a dominant role.

Varieties of culture

The strength of a culture will clearly influence its impact on corporate behaviour. Strong cultures will have more widely shared, and more clearly expressed beliefs and values. These values will probably have been developed over a considerable period of time and they will be perceived as functional in the sense that they help the organization to achieve its purpose.

There may be one culture pervading the organization, but there will almost certainly be a number of sub-cultures in different departments, functions or divisions. This can complicate culture management because of possible inconsistencies or conflicts between cultures.

In fact, an important question to answer when considering cultural change is the extent to which a common culture should be developed (or imposed) throughout the organization, or the degree to which strategic business units should continue to maintain their own distinctive cultures.

The answer to this question will depend on the philosophy of top management, which in turn will affect and be affected by the nature of the organization and its operation. In each of Goold and Campbell's (1986) categories of strategic planning, financial control and strategic control companies, different approaches will be used.

Culture may also be strongly influenced by different product–market conditions or different technologies. In Book Club Associates, for example, the culture in its London office, where business was generated through marketing and advertising activities, was flexible, innovative and informal. It was quite different from the culture in its Swindon operational division, which was essentially a paper factory and was therefore much more disciplined, rigid and formal.

The more operational responsibility is devolved, the less pressure there will be from the centre to adopt a common culture on the assumption that success at the devolved level is more important than cultural consistency. In other words, what matters is 'what you achieve rather than how you achieve it'.

The companies with the strongest and most pervasive cultures such as Hewlett-Packard, Marks and Spencer or IBM are likely to be those which are well established and operationally homogeneous in the sense that they practice low levels of business as distinct from product diversification. In Peters and Waterman's (1982) phrase, they 'stick to their knitting'.

Implications

Culture is developed and manifests itself in different ways in different organizations. It is not possible to say that one culture is better than another, only that it is dissimilar in certain ways. There is no such thing as an ideal culture, only an appropriate culture. This means that there can be no universal prescription for managing culture, although there are certain approaches which can be helpful, as described in the next section.

APPROACHES TO CULTURE MANAGEMENT

Culture management is about reinforcing or embedding an existing functional culture or changing a dysfunctional culture. The approach will be affected by certain overall considerations as discussed below. With these in mind, culture management is a matter of analysis and diagnosis, followed by the application of appropriate reinforcement or change levers.

Overall considerations

Schein (1987) has suggested that the most powerful primary mechanisms for culture embedding and reinforcement are:

- what leaders pay attention to, measure and control;
- leaders' reactions to critical incidents and crises;
- deliberate role modelling, teaching and coaching by leaders;
- criteria for allocation of rewards and status;
- criteria for recruitment, selection, promotion and commitment.

Because cultures have evolved over the years and are usually deeply rooted, they are difficult to change. It is very hard to get people to alter long-held attitudes and beliefs, and attempts to do so often fail. All you can do is to get them to alter their behaviour in ways which will reduce dysfunctional elements in the culture and support the introduction of functional elements.

But changing behaviour is not always easy, although it will happen in traumatic circumstances such as a crisis, a change in ownership or the arrival of a powerful, autocratic, charismatic and visionary leader.

Analysis and diagnosis

The analysis of culture and the diagnosis of what management action needs to be taken can be carried out on a continuous basis by observation and noting behaviours which indicate the values and norms prevalent in the organization.

A more searching analysis would use instruments such as interviews, questionnaires, focus groups (representative groups of employees whose views are sought on organizational or work issues), attitude surveys and workshops.

Culture management programmes

One or more of the following approaches can be used to help in managing culture.

1   The issue of mission and value statements which state explicitly where the organization is going and the values it adopts in getting there – but

these statements must represent reality and must be followed up by workshops, training and discussions which translate the words into deeds.

2   Workshops to get people involved in discussing new values and ways of behaviour and practising their application; as in the British Airways 'Putting People First' programme which involved all 38,000 staff attending an intensive three-day workshop, encouraging them to think about and accept the importance of customer service.

3   Education and training programmes to extend knowledge and teach people new skills.

4   Performance management programmes which ensure through the mechanisms of objective setting and performance appraisal that the values, norms and behaviours which the cultural change programme is developing are absorbed and acted upon as part of the normal process of management.

5   Reward management systems which reward people for behaviour that is in accord with the values built into the culture change programme.

Such programmes can be used not only to change, but also to reinforce a culture. Ideally, they should be conducted on an organization-wide basis but it may have to be recognized that different parts of the organization can legitimately have different cultures and that it could be counterproductive to impose an alien culture upon them.

Individual managers can make a vital contribution by, first, understanding their culture, secondly, getting involved as far as possible in the definition of the aims and constituents of a culture management programme and, finally, playing their part by practising the required behaviour themselves, developing it in their staff, and instilling or reinforcing the value system of the organization throughout their department.

THE ROLE OF THE HUMAN RESOURCE SPECIALIST IN CULTURE MANAGEMENT

Human resource specialists are in a good position to analyze the existing culture and to produce diagnoses to top management on what needs to be done about it. They can advise management on the drafting of value statements, on how these can be communicated to employees and on how behaviour can be modified so that it is aligned with the changed values.

Importantly, human resource specialists can design and help to implement change management programmes, especially those involving education and training, performance management and reward management initiatives.

The human resource specialist as an internal consultant

The role of human resource specialists is extended in many organizations in the direction of internal consultancy on issues concerning culture management, as well as the introduction of new HRM systems. External consultants are still used frequently because they can take a detached view, but they are more likely to be operating as part of a joint management and personnel specialist team rather than entirely independently, as in the old organization development or 'OD' days.

Process consultancy

The facilitator of a culture management programme will often use process consultancy methods. Process consulting is a collaborative approach in which the consultant is involved with members of the organization in gathering information, analyzing and diagnosing needs and problems, obtaining agreement to courses of action and, as described in Chapter 7, cultivating commitment to change.

Process consulting, as described by Schein (1969), requires the external consultant, or internal HR specialist if carrying out this role, to:

■ get people to share in the process of analyzing and reformulating different interpretations of the requirements or problems in their context;
■ provide clients with insight into the situation – its main features, the factors affecting it, and the various processes or human actions which occur in the normal flow of work, in the conduct of meetings and in formal and informal encounters between members of the organization;
■ provide new and challenging alternatives for clients to consider but *not* ready-made 'expert' solutions;
■ help people to structure their thoughts so that logical, coherent and practical solutions to problems emerge from the process;
■ act as a catalyst and adviser, not as a group leader;
■ intervene if the group does not appear to be adopting a sufficiently rigorous approach to analysis and diagnosis;
■ listen and observe, and not talk too much;
■ help the group to become aware of the decisions it has made and the methods it has used to make them;
■ do everything he or she can to get the group to feel it 'owns' the solution or course of action;
■ ensure that decisions are noted and fed back to the right people, and that plans are made to implement them.

Process consultancy requires considerable skill. Rapport has to be established with staff at all levels. The HR specialist as consultant has to be able to observe and analyze the processes at work in the organization, and probe, listen and work effectively with groups. The process consultant has to be perceived as independent and this may be difficult where the HR specialist has other personnel responsibilities which identify him or her with management. However, even if it is not possible to take on the full process consulting role, HR specialists can still make an important contribution as facilitators or change agents, using their expertise in applying process consultancy skills.

Part III

HRM Processes

Chapter 7

Change Management

HRM is largely about helping to achieve change. Its introduction and development may require significant alterations to the organization's culture and to its policies, structure and systems. When HRM is in place, its strategies and processes must be responsive and adaptive to change.

An HRM approach to the management of change will recognize that the key to success lies not only in a transformational leader, supported by powerful change mechanisms, but also by understanding that change is implemented by people and that it is their behaviour and support that count. The most important aim of change management is to achieve commitment to change.

Change management in an HRM setting is based on a strategic view of where the organization, or any part of it, is going and how its human resources can help it to get there. Successful change management requires an understanding of:

■ the main types of change;
■ how change affects individuals;
■ the process of change;
■ prescriptions for change management;
■ how to build commitment to change;
■ the role of leadership in achieving change;
■ the role of the HR specialist in facilitating change.

TYPES OF CHANGE

There are two main types of change: strategic and operational.

Strategic change

Strategic change is concerned with broad, long-term and organization-wide issues. It is about moving to a future state which has been defined generally in terms of strategic vision and scope. It will cover the purpose and mission of the organization, its corporate philosophy on such matters as growth, quality, innovation and values concerning people, the customer needs served and the technologies employed. This overall definition leads to specifications of competitive positioning, and strategic goals for achieving and maintaining competitive advantage and for product–market development. These goals are supported by policies concerning marketing, sales, manufacturing, product and process development, finance and human resource management.

Strategic change takes place within the context of the external competitive, economic and social environment, and in relation to the organization's internal resources, capabilities, culture, structure and systems. Its successful implementation requires thorough analysis and understanding of these factors in the formulation and planning stages. The ultimate achievement of sustainable competitive advantage relies on the two qualities defined by Pettigrew and Whipp (1991):

> The capacity of the firm to identify and understand the competitive forces in play and how they change over time, linked to the competence of a business to mobilize and manage the resources necessary for the chosen competitive response through time.

Strategic change, however, should not be treated simplistically as a straightforward and sequential process of getting from A to B, which can be planned and executed as a logical sequence of events. Pettigrew and Whipp (1991) issued the following warning based on their research into competitiveness and managing change in the motor, financial services, insurance and publishing industries:

> The process by which strategic changes are made seldom move directly through neat, successive stages of analysis, choice and implementation. Changes in the firm's environment persistently threaten the course and logic of strategic changes: dilemma abounds. ... We conclude that one of the defining features of the process, in so far as management action is concerned, is ambiguity; seldom is there an easily isolated logic to strategic change. Instead, that process may derive its motive force from an amalgam of economic, personal and political imperatives. Their introduction through time requires that those responsible for managing that process make continual assessments, repeated choices and multiple adjustments.

Operational change

Operational change relates to new systems, procedures, structures or technology which will have an immediate effect on working arrangements within a part of the organization. But their impact on people can be more significant than broader strategic change and they have to be handled just as carefully.

HOW PEOPLE CHANGE

The ways in which people change are best explained by reference to social cognitive theory as developed by Bandura (1986). The assumptions of this theory are that:

- people make conscious choices about their behaviours;
- the information people use to make their choices comes from their environment;
- their choices are based upon
  — the things that are important to them
  — the views they have about their own abilities to behave in certain ways
  — the consequences they think will follow whatever behaviour they decide to engage in.

For those concerned in change management, the implications of this theory are that:

- the tighter the link between a particular behaviour and a particular outcome, the more likely it is that we will engage in that behaviour;
- the more desirable the outcome, the more likely it is that we will engage in behaviour that we believe will lead to it;
- the more confident we are that we can actually assume a new behaviour, the more likely we are to try it.

To change people's behaviour, therefore, we have first to change the environment within which they work, secondly, to convince them that the new behaviour is something they can accomplish (training is important) and, thirdly, to persuade them that it will lead to an outcome that they will value. None of these steps is easy. To achieve them, it helps to know more about the process of change.

THE PROCESS OF CHANGE

Change, as Kanter (1989) puts it, is the process of analyzing 'the past to elicit the present actions required for the future'. It involves moving from a present state, through a transition state to a future desired state.

The process starts with an awareness of the need for change. An analysis of this state and the factors that have created it leads to a diagnosis of the distinctive characteristics of the situation, and an indication of the direction in which action needs to be taken. Possible courses of action can then be identified and evaluated, and a choice made of the preferred action.

It is then necessary to decide how to get from here to there. Managing the change process in this transition state is a critical phase in the change process. It is here that the problems of introducing change emerge and have to be managed. These problems can include resistance to change, low stability, high levels of stress, misdirected energy, conflict and losing momentum, hence the need to do everything possible to anticipate reactions and likely impediments to the smooth introduction of change.

The installation stage can also be painful. When planning change there is a tendency for people to think that it will be an entirely logical and linear affair. It is not like that at all. As described by Pettigrew and Whipp (1991), the implementation of change is an 'iterative, cumulative and reformulation-in-use process'.

PRESCRIPTIONS FOR CHANGE

There have been many prescriptions for managing change. The following is a description of the more interesting ones.

Kurt Lewin (1951)

Kurt Lewin defined the mechanisms for managing change as follows.

- *Unfreezing* – altering the present stable equilibrium which supports existing behaviours and attitudes. This process must take account of the inherent threats change presents to people and the need to motivate those affected to attain the natural state of equilibrium by accepting change.
- *Changing* – developing new responses based on new information.
- *Refreezing* – stabilizing the change by introducing the new responses into the personalities of those concerned.

He proposed a method which he called 'field force analysis' to assess the forces which are likely to resist change, as well as those which have created the need for change. The steps required are to:

- analyze the restraining or driving forces which will affect the transition to the future state – these restraining forces will include the reactions of those who see change as unnecessary or constituting a threat;
- assess which of the driving or restraining forces are critical;
- take steps both to increase the critical driving forces and to decrease the critical restraining forces.

Richard Beckhard (1969)

Richard Beckhard stated that the need for change may be stimulated by external demands or forces which compel management to act – they have no choice. In other cases, the need for change is stimulated by forces either within or outside the organization, but nevertheless under management's general control. External forces include worldwide competition, changes in market demand, availability of resources, development of new technology, and legislative and social priorities. In many technology-based industries, the pressure for change comes from within:

> Traditionally, technical workers, even professionally trained engineers, have accepted relatively structured roles, responsibilities and

procedures as given. Now these 'knowledge workers' are demanding increased autonomy and responsibility in defining their work, more flexibility in work hours, rules and procedures, and greater opportunities for achievement recognition.

Beckhard's prescription for change management comprised the following steps.

1 Diagnose the problem that necessitates a change.

2 Set goals and define the future state or organizational conditions desired after the change.

3 Define the transition state activities and commitments required to reach the future state.

4 Develop strategies and action plans for managing this transition.

But he pointed out that change management is not a neat sequential process. The initial tasks of defining the future state and assessing present conditions demand simultaneous attention.

Valerie Stewart (1983)

Valerie Stewart supports an incremental approach to change, given time. This means that the need for change has to be anticipated. She recommends that the opinion leaders in the groups you want to change should be identified. She also suggests that there is plenty of evidence to show that if you want to change people's attitudes, rather than making a full-blooded assault on their attitudes as such, it is better to try to create the circumstances in which they behave as if the attitude change has happened: 'Then they find out that it's not so bad after all and the attitude alters to conform to the new behaviour'. If you combine behavioural change actions with the incremental approach, attitude change will creep along somewhere behind until it reaches a critical mass, after which major changes may occur in the structure of the attitudes themselves.

Her final advice to those concerned in change management is that:

To manage change you need to be able to be a voice in the wilderness and you need to get your timing right. Almost by definition, a small touch on the tiller is better than a massive heave in mid-course, but to make that small touch you need the farsightedness which other people around you might not share, and the sense of timing which tells you how much pressure to apply, and where, and when.

Rosabeth Moss Kanter (1984 and 1989)

In *The Change Masters* (1984), Rosabeth Moss Kanter highlights the environmental and leadership factors in her analysis of change. She believes that organizational change is stimulated by management's perceptions of the environment rather than the actual environmental pressures – they 'enact' them by defining selectively certain things as important. Organizational change consists of 'a series of emerging constructions of reality, including revision of the past, to correspond to the requisites of new players and new demands'.

Kanter suggests that the key factors to take into account in managing change are relevant information, appropriate resources and expert support to those involved in the change process. And the action vehicles for change will be integrating and institutionalizing mechanisms.

She recommends a realistic approach to change – 'don't try and do too much all at once', and quotes with approval a chief executive's statement that 'a working compromise is better than an optimal solution, poorly implemented'.

In a later work, *When Giants Learn to Dance* (1989), Kanter concentrates on the instability of the environment and the need to develop more focused and flexible organizations. This means rejecting bureaucratic approaches and minimizing adversarial relationships with stakeholders. The culture of the organization must stress the need for synergy and 'stakeholder partnerships'.

Tom Peters (1988)

In *Thriving on Chaos*, Tom Peters advocated an approach to change management based on his view that we are in an era of unprecedented instability and uncertainty: 'Predictability is a thing of the past'. His prescription is that leaders at all levels must become obsessive about change, which should become the norm. He emphasizes that: 'The most efficient and effective route to bold change is the participation of everyone, every day, in incremental change'. The road to it is paved with 'a million experiments, a million false steps – and the wholehearted participation of everyone'.

John Harvey-Jones (1988)

In *Making it Happen*, John Harvey-Jones wrote that: 'Management is about change, and maintaining a high rate of change'. His comments on managing change were as follows.

- Always remember that the engine of change is dissatisfaction with the present, and the brakes of change are fear of the unknown and fear of the future.
- People should be asking not whether you are going to change, but how long before you do so.
- People should not only be aware of the need for change, but also of the high risk involved in not changing.

■ The task of leadership is to make the status quo more dangerous than launching into the unknown.
■ The sense of pride in the achievements of one's team can be a force for change.
■ In the process of change, small actions can have a tremendous catalytic effect.
■ It is an absolute responsibility of the business organization to look after those who cannot adapt to change.
■ 'The objectives and the company have to be seen to be decent to command the freely given spirit which will build an enduring organization, and an enduring organization is one which is able to adapt continuously not only to the needs of today, but also to the needs of tomorrow. That is why change management is such a vital skill to be learned.'

Charles Handy (1989)

In *The Age of Unreason*, Charles Handy emphasized that change is about learning. It is a reframing process which requires the ability to see things in other ways, and this may require the displacement of concepts – taking concepts from one field and transferring them to another in order to gain insights.

Handy suggests that change is dependent on the organization's climate and that the aim should be to develop its capacity to learn.

Richard Pascale (1990)

In *Managing on the Edge*, Richard Pascale states that disequilibrium might be a better strategy for survival than order. Change can be discontinuous and internal differences can widen the spectrum of an organization's options by generating new points of view; he quotes Weick's (1977) remarks:

The more one delves into the subtleties of organizations, the more one begins to question what order means and the more concerned one becomes that prevailing preconceptions of order (that which is efficient, planned, predictable and has survived) are suspect. Simply pushing harder within the old boundaries will not do.

Pascale advocates the development of new paradigms or mindsets on the principle that 'nothing fails like success' – businesses and people can too easily become too complacent. His overall prescription is that:

a system requires 'internal variety' to cope with external change.... Internal difference can widen the spectrum of an organization's options by generating new points of view. This in turn can produce disequilibrium: under these conditions, self-renewal and adaptation occur.

Beer, Eisenstat and Spector (1990)

The starting point of Beer, Eisenstat and Spector's *Harvard Business Review* article, 'Why change programs don't produce change', is that most such programmes are guided by a theory of change which is fundamentally flawed. This theory states that changes in attitudes lead to changes in behaviour. 'According to this model, change is like a conversion experience. Once people "get religion", changes in their behaviour will surely follow.'

They believe that this theory gets the change process exactly backwards:

> In fact, individual behaviour is powerfully shaped by the organiza-
> tional roles people play. The most effective way to change behaviour,
> therefore, is to put people into a new organizational context, which
> imposes new roles, responsibilities and relationships on them. This
> creates a situation that in a sense 'forces' new attitudes and
> behaviour on people.

They prescribe six steps to effective change which concentrate on 'task alignment' – reorganizing employees' roles, responsibilities and relationships to solve specific business problems in small units where goals and tasks can be clearly defined. The aim of the following overlapping steps is to build a self-reinforcing cycle of commitment, coordination and competence. The steps are as follows.

1 Mobilize commitment to change through the joint analysis of business problems.

2 Develop a shared vision of how to organize and manage for competitiveness.

3 Foster consensus for the new vision, competence to enact it and cohesion to move it along.

4 Spread revitalization to all departments without pushing it from the top – don't force the issue, let each department find its own way to the new organization.

5 Institutionalize revitalization through formal policies, systems and structures.

6 Monitor and adjust strategies in response to problems in the revitaliza-tion process.

Andrew Pettigrew and Richard Whipp (1991)

Following their research into change management and competitive success in seven British firms, Pettigrew and Whipp suggested the following 'conditional features' for strategic change.

- Build a climate within the firm which will be receptive to change. This involves justifying why change should take place.
- Build the capacity to mount the change before attempting to introduce it.
- Establish a change agenda which not only sets the direction of the business, but also establishes the necessary visions and values.

They also suggested the following secondary measures to support strategic interventions.

- Break down intentions to actionable components.
- Allocate responsibility for these components to change managers who operate within appropriate structures and at various levels in the organization.
- Support clear and exacting target setting by rethought communication mechanisms and adjusted reward systems.

Don Young (1992)

In an article on 'Change and the personnel manager' Don Young identifies four change strategies.

1 *Transformation* – this is appropriate for organizations which have the vision and foresight to recognize large opportunities (or threats) and are prepared radically to change what they do and how they do it.

2 *Crisis management* – this strategy is forced upon organizations threatened with bankruptcy, catastrophic failure or acquisition which need the quickest possible 'fixes' to survive and then move ahead again.

3 *Fine tuning* – this is for organizations which are successful and effective in relatively stable environments, but which sensibly pursue a strategy of continuous improvement.

4 *Building* – this is practised by organizations which have a well-established and successful business formula and a well-developed organization, and wish to extend the scope of the business progressively over relatively long time-scales.

On the basis of his experience as a personnel director, Young believes that the key elements in an effective and sustainable change process are:

- a deep consensus among the top team about the context the business is in and what needs to be done to achieve sustainable good performance;
- an understanding of the change strategy the organization should pursue now, and how this may alter over time;
- a deep and broad 'feel' for the organization – how it works, what it is like, what needs to be changed, and what should be preserved and sustained;

- an understanding of the appropriate 'levers' – (processes, actions, communications, interventions) which can be used to direct and manage a change process;
- people in leadership positions who are suited by temperament and skills to the particular change strategy being pursued.

Guidelines for change

It is possible to distil from the collective wisdom of these writers and the author's own practical experiences as a consultant and a general manager the following guidelines for change.

- The achievement of sustainable change requires strong commitment and leadership from the top.
- Understanding is necessary of the culture of the organization and the levers for change which are most likely to be effective in that culture.
- Those concerned with managing change at all levels should have the temperament and leadership skills appropriate to the circumstances of the organization and its change strategies.
- It is important to build a working environment which is conducive to change. This means developing the firm as a 'learning organization' (see Chapter 13).
- Change will be introduced more effectively if it is seen by all concerned as being an integral part of an overall corporate strategy.
- Although there may be an overall strategy for change, it is best tackled incrementally (except in crisis conditions). The change programme should be broken down into actionable segments for which people can be held accountable.
- The reward system should encourage innovation and recognize success in achieving change.
- Change implies streams of activity across time and 'may require the enduring of abortive efforts or the build up of slow incremental phases of adjustment which then allow short bursts of incremental action to take place' (Pettigrew and Whipp 1991).
- Change will always involve failure as well as success. The failures must be expected and learned from.
- Hard evidence and data on the need for change are the most powerful tools for its achievement, but establishing the need for change is easier than deciding how to satisfy it.
- It is easier to change behaviour by changing process, structure and systems, than to change attitudes or the corporate culture.
- There are always people in organizations who welcome the challenges and opportunities that change can provide. They are the ones to be chosen as change agents.
- Middle managers are the people who will be most involved in managing change. They have to be convinced that it is necessary (not

always easy) and should be given ample training, help and encouragement.

■ Resistance to change is inevitable if the individuals concerned feel that they are going to be worse off – implicitly or explicitly. The inept management of change will produce that reaction.

■ In an age of global competition, technological innovation, turbulence, discontinuity, even chaos, change is inevitable and necessary. The organization must do all it can to explain why change is essential and how it will affect everyone. Moreover, every effort must be made to protect the interests of those affected by change.

■ Continuous attention must be paid not only to communicating the reasons for change, but also to listening to and acting upon the reactions of those concerned.

To summarize, the ingredients of a successful change process are:

■ top-level commitment, clearly and visibly evident to all staff;
■ full involvement and commitment on the part of middle managers who will be the chief agents of change;
■ systematic and reinforcing communication – two ways – with staff so that key messages are fully understood;
■ consistency with other major change projects with clear explanations of how they will fit the overarching business strategy.

GAINING COMMITMENT TO CHANGE

These guidelines point in one direction: having decided why changes are necessary, what the goals are and how they are to be achieved, the most important task is to gain the commitment of all concerned to the proposed change.

A strategy for gaining commitment to change should cover the following phases.

Preparation

In this first phase, the person or persons likely to be affected by the proposed change are contacted in order to be made aware of the fact that a change is being contemplated.

Acceptance

In the second phase, information is provided on the purpose of the change, how it is proposed to implement it and what effect it will have on those concerned. The aim is to achieve understanding of what the change means and to obtain a positive reaction. This is more likely if:

■ the change is perceived to be consistent with the mission and values of the organization;

- the change is not thought to be threatening;
- the change seems likely to meet the needs of those concerned;
- there is a compelling and fully understood reason for change;
- those concerned are involved in planning and implementing the change programme on the principle that people support what they help to create;
- it is understood that steps will be taken to mitigate any detrimental effects of the change.

It may be difficult, even impossible, to meet these requirements. That is why the problems of gaining commitment to change should not be underestimated.

During this phase, the extent to which reactions are positive or negative can be noted and action taken accordingly.

It is at this stage that original plans may have to be modified to cater for legitimate reservations or second thoughts. As Pettigrew and Whipp (1991) concluded from their research, implementing change 'may include clusters of iterative action in order to break through ignorance or resistance'.

Commitment

During the third phase, the change is implemented and becomes operational. The change process and people's reaction to it need to be monitored. There will inevitably be delays, setbacks, unforeseen problems and negative reactions from those faced with the reality of change. A response to these reactions is essential so that valid criticisms can be acted upon or explanations given of why it is believed that the change should proceed as planned.

Following implementation, the aim is to get the change adopted as, with use, its worth becomes evident. The decision is made at this stage on whether to continue with the change, or whether it needs to be modified or even aborted. Account should again be taken of the views of those involved.

Finally, and after further modifications, as required, the change is institutionalized and becomes an inherent part of the organization's culture and operations.

THE ROLE OF LEADERSHIP IN MANAGING CHANGE

Change demands leadership which creates and directs energy at all levels in the organization. As Kotter (1980) has written:

Management is about coping with complexity, leadership is about coping with change. Leaders create visions and strategies and these first describe a business, technology or corporate culture in terms of what it should become, and then articulate a means of achieving these goals.

As Kanter (1984) put it:

> The skill of corporate leaders, the ultimate change masters, lies in their ability to envision a new reality and aid in its translation into concrete terms.

There has to be someone to set the direction, and when strategic change is required, that someone will be at the top of the organization. But leaders cannot go it alone and the process of leadership will incorporate a stream of relationships over time, as the leader enlists support and initiates action to be carried out by other people.

There will be leaders at all levels in the organization and in each function or unit of the firm. Top management has the task of mobilizing, directing and coordinating their efforts to achieve sustainable change. This will be an iterative process. The leader's vision and strategy will have to be modified over time to meet new situations, and to respond to the views of other people.

There is no single style of leadership which will gain commitment to change. In one sense, it clearly has to be transformational leadership, but how the leader behaves in effecting the transformation will be influenced by the situation, and effective leaders are able to modify their style to meet changing requirements. As Pettigrew and Whipp (1991) established:

> Leading change in order to compete is not understood by reference to universal principles carried out by an exceptional individual. More effective in leading change appears to be the use of varying leadership approaches over time; a combination of practices to address shifting competitive circumstances; the recognition that leader and context will affect each other reciprocally; and the use of cperational leaders at all levels in the firm.

THE ROLE OF THE HUMAN RESOURCE SPECIALIST

Human resource specialists, particularly if they are part of the top management team and have the ear of the chief executive, can exert a major influence on change. Their influence will be strongest if they have an understanding of the processes, systems, interventions, media and interactions which are the levers for change, and can relate this understanding to an appreciation of the culture, and the key business and people issues affecting the organization.

Human resource specialists can facilitate the process of change management if they:

■ intervene to point out where change is required;

- help in the articulation of an agenda for change which takes account of all contextual considerations, especially their human aspects;
- analyze how people might react to change;
- advise on how the change agenda should be communicated in a way which will minimize resistance to change;
- facilitate workshops and other means of getting people involved in analyzing the reasons for change, deciding what changes should take place and discussing how it should be implemented;
- advise on and manage the education and training programmes required to ensure that employees have the knowledge and skills to introduce change and operate new systems.

Chapter 8

Commitment

The concept of commitment plays an important part in HRM philosophy. As Guest (1987) has indicated, HRM policies are designed to 'maximize organizational integration, employee commitment, flexibility and quality of work'. This chapter explores the measuring and significance of organizational commitment, considers certain problems about the concept and discusses how it can be developed.

THE MEANING OF ORGANIZATIONAL COMMITMENT

Commitment refers to attachment and loyalty. As defined by Porter *et al* (1974), commitment is the relative strength of the individual's identification with, and involvement in, a particular organization. It consists of these three factors.

1   A strong desire to remain a member of the organization.

2   A strong belief in, and acceptance of, the values and goals of the organization.

3   A readiness to exert considerable effort on behalf of the organization.

An alternative, although closely related, definition of commitment emphasizes the importance of behaviour in creating commitment. As Salancik (1977) put it 'commitment is a state of being in which an individual becomes bound by his actions to beliefs that sustain his activities and his own involvement'.

Three features of behaviour are important in binding individuals to their acts: the visibility of the acts; the extent to which the outcomes are irrevocable; and the degree to which the person undertakes the action voluntarily. Commitment, according to Salancik, can be increased and harnessed 'to obtain support for organizational ends and interests' through such ploys as participation in decisions about actions.

THE SIGNIFICANCE OF COMMITMENT

Organizations facing increased competition, and coping with change and turbulence, are more anxious than ever before to get people to identify more closely with their objectives and values. In many ways, organizations are becoming more fragmented and Drucker (1988) has posed the question: 'How do we get unified vision in an organization peopled with specialists?'

There have been two schools of thought about commitment. One, the 'from control to commitment' school, was led by Walton (1985a and b), who saw commitment strategy as a more rewarding approach to human resource management, in contrast to the traditional control strategy. The other, 'Japanese/excellence' school, is represented by writers such as Pascale and Athos (1981) and Peters and Waterman (1982), who looked at the Japanese model and related the achievement of excellence to getting the wholehearted commitment of the workforce to the organization.

From control to commitment

The importance of commitment was highlighted by Walton (1985a). His theme was that improved performance would result if the organization moved away from the traditional control-oriented approach to workforce management, which relies upon establishing order, exercising control and 'achieving efficiency in the application of the workforce'. He argued that this approach should be replaced by a commitment strategy. He suggested that workers respond best – and most creatively – not when they are tightly controlled by management, placed in narrowly defined jobs, and treated like an unwelcome necessity, but, instead, when they are given broader responsibilities, encouraged to contribute and helped to achieve satisfaction in their work.

Walton suggested that in the new commitment-based approach:

> Jobs are designed to be broader than before, to combine planning and implementation, and to include efforts to upgrade operations, not just to maintain them. Individual responsibilities are expected to change as conditions change, and teams, not individuals, often are the organizational units accountable for performance. With management hierarchies relatively flat and differences in status minimized, control and lateral coordination depend on shared goals. And expertise rather than formal position determines influence.

Put like this, a commitment strategy does not sound like a crude attempt to manipulate people to accept management's values and goals. In fact, Walton does not describe it as being instrumental in this manner. His prescription is for a broad HRM approach to the ways in which people are treated, jobs are designed and organizations are managed. And he quotes a number of examples in America where unions have cooperated with management; talking about common interests and agreeing to sponsor quality-of-working-life programmes and employee involvement activities.

The approach recommended by Walton is a convincing method of dealing with Drucker's question.

The Japanese/excellence school

Attempts made to explain the secret of Japanese business success by such writers as Ouchi (1981) and Pascale and Athos (1981) led to the theory that the best way to motivate people is to get their full commitment to the values of the organization by leadership and involvement. This might be called the 'hearts and minds' approach to motivation and, among other things, it popularized such devices as quality circles.

The baton was taken up by Peters and Waterman (1982) and their imitators later in the 1980s. This approach to excellence was summed up by Peters and Austin (1985) when they wrote:

> Trust people and treat them like adults, enthuse them by lively and imaginative leadership, develop and demonstrate an obsession for quality, make them feel they own the business, and your workforce will respond with total commitment.

PROBLEMS WITH THE CONCEPT OF COMMITMENT

A number of commentators have raised questions about the concept of commitment. These relate to three main problem areas: 1) its unitary frame of reference; 2) commitment as an inhibitor of flexibility; and 3) whether high commitment does, in practice, result in improved organizational performance.

Unitary frame of reference

A comment frequently made about the concept of commitment is that it is too simplistic in adopting a unitary frame of reference; in other words, it assumes unrealistically that an organization consists of people with shared interests. It has been suggested by people like Cyert and March (1963), Mangham (1979) and Mintzberg (1983) that an organization is really a coalition of interest groups where political processes are an inevitable part of everyday life. The pluralistic perspective recognizes the legitimacy of different interests and values, and therefore asks the question 'Commitment to what?' Thus, as Coopey and Hartley (1991) put it 'commitment is not an all-or-nothing affair (though many managers might like it to be) but a question of multiple or competing commitments for the individual'.

Legge (1989) also raises this question in her discussion of strong culture as a key requirement of HRM:

> 'Strong culture' is aimed at uniting employees through a shared set of managerially sanctioned values ('quality', 'service', 'innovation' etc) that assume an identification of employees and employer interests. Such co-optation – through cultural management of course – reinforces the intention that autonomy will be exercised responsibly, ie in management's interests.

Presumably, Legge is not implying that managerial values for quality, service and innovation are necessarily wrong *because* they are managerial values. But it is not unreasonable to believe that pursuing a value such as innovation could work against the interests of employees by, for example, resulting in redundancies. And it would be quite reasonable for any employee encouraged to behave in accordance with a value supported by management to ask 'What's in it for me?'.

Commitment and flexibility

It was pointed out by Coopey and Hartley (1991) that:

> The problem for a unitarist notion of organizational commitment is that it fosters a conformist approach which not only fails to reflect organizational reality, but can be narrowing and limiting for the organization.

They argue that if employees are expected and encouraged to commit themselves tightly to a single set of values and goals, they will not be able to cope with the ambiguities and uncertainties which are endemic in organizational life in times of change. Conformity to 'imposed' values will inhibit creative problem solving, and high commitment to present courses of action will increase both resistance to change and the stress which invariably occurs when change takes place.

If commitment is related to tightly defined plans, then this will become a real problem. To avoid it, the emphasis should be on overall strategic directions. These would be communicated to staff with the proviso that changing circumstances will require their amendment. In the meantime, however, everyone can at least be informed, in general terms, where the organization is heading and, more specifically, the part they are expected to play in helping the organization to get there.

Values need not necessarily be restrictive. They can be defined in ways which allow for freedom of choice within broad guidelines. In fact, the values themselves can refer to such processes as flexibility, innovation and responsiveness to change. Thus, far from inhibiting creative problem solving, they can encourage it.

The impact of high commitment

A belief in the positive value of commitment has been confidently expressed by Walton (1985a):

Underlying all these (human resource) policies is a management philosophy, often embedded in a published statement, that acknowledges the legitimate claims of a company's multiple stakeholders – owners, employees, customers and the public. At the centre of this philosophy is a belief that eliciting employee commitment will lead to enhanced performance. The evidence shows this belief to be well founded.

However, a review by Guest (1991) of the mainly North American literature, reinforced by the limited UK research available, revealed that: 'High organizational commitment is associated with lower labour turnover and absence, but there is no clear link to performance'.

It is probably wise not to expect too much from commitment as a means of making a direct and immediate impact on performance. It is not the same as motivation. Commitment is a wider concept and tends to be more stable over a period of time and less responsive to transitory aspects of an employee's job. It is possible to be dissatisfied with a particular feature of a job, while retaining a reasonably high level of commitment to the organization as a whole.

In relating commitment to motivation it is useful to distinguish, as do Buchanan and Huczynski (1985), three perspectives.

1   The goals towards which people aim. From this perspective, goals such as the good of the company, or effective performance at work, may provide a degree of motivation for some employees, who could be regarded as committed, in so far as they feel they own the goals.

2   The process by which goals and objectives at work are selected, which is quite distinct from the way in which commitment arises within individuals.

3   The social process of motivating others to perform effectively. From this viewpoint, strategies aimed at increasing motivation also affect commitment. It may be true to say that, where commitment is present, motivation is likely to be strong, particularly if a long-term view is taken of effective performance.

It seems reasonable to believe that strong commitment to work is likely to result in conscientious and self-directed application to do the job, regular attendance, nominal supervision and a high level of effort. Commitment to the organization will certainly be related to the intention to stay – in other words, loyalty to the company.

CREATING COMMITMENT

In spite of these reservations, it is difficult to deny that it is desirable for management to have defined strategic goals and values. And it is equally desirable from management's point of view for employees to behave in ways which support these strategies and values.

But in enlisting this support, account should be taken of the reservations discussed above. First, it has to be accepted that the interests of the organization and of its members do not necessarily coincide. It can be asserted by management that everyone will benefit from organizational success in terms of security, pay, opportunities for advancement etc. But employees and their trade unions may be difficult to convince that this is the case if they believe that the success is to be achieved by such actions as disinvestments, downsizing, cost reductions affecting pay and employment, tougher performance standards or tighter management controls. And when defining values, it is important to spell out how the organization intends to fulfil its responsibilities to *all* its stakeholders, especially employees. And these values have to be acted upon.

Secondly, management must not define and communicate values in such a way as to inhibit flexibility, creativity and the ability to adapt to change. Strategies have to be defined in broad terms with caveats that they will be amended if circumstances change. Values have to emphasize the need for flexibility, innovation and teamworking, as well as the need for performance and quality.

Thirdly, too much should not be expected from campaigns to increase commitment. They may reduce labour turnover, increase identification with the company and develop feelings of loyalty among its employees. They may increase job satisfaction, but there is no evidence that higher levels of job satisfaction necessarily improve performance. They may provide a context within which motivation, and therefore performance, will increase. But there is no guarantee that this will take place, although the chances of gaining improvements will be increased if the campaign is focused upon a specific value such as quality.

It may be naïve to believe that 'hearts and minds' campaigns to win commitment will transform organizational behaviour overnight. But it is surely useful for organizations to do what they can along the lines described below to influence behaviour, to support the achievement of objectives and to uphold values that are inherently worth while. It is good management practice to define its expectations in terms of objectives and standards of performance. It is even better management practice to discuss and agree these objectives and standards with employees.

Steps to create commitment will be concerned with both strategic goals and values. They may include communication, education and training programmes, initiatives to increase involvement and 'ownership', and the development of performance and reward management systems.

Communication programmes

It seems to be strikingly obvious that commitment will only be gained if people understand what they are expected to be committed to. But managements too often fail to pay sufficient attention to delivering the message in terms which recognize that the frame of reference for those who receive it is likely to be quite different from their own. Management's expectations will not necessarily coincide with those of employees. Pluralism prevails. And, in delivering the message, the use of different and complementary channels of communication such as newsletters, briefing groups, videos, notice boards etc is often neglected.

Education

Education is another form of communication. An educational programme is designed to increase both knowledge and understanding of, for example, total quality management. The aim will be to influence behaviour and thereby progressively change attitudes.

Training

Training is designed to develop specific competences. For example, if one of the values to be supported is flexibility, it will be necessary to extend the range of skills possessed by members of work teams through multi-skilling programmes.

Commitment is enhanced if managers can gain the confidence and respect of their teams, and training to improve the quality of management should form an important part of any programme for increasing commitment. Management training can also be focused on increasing the competence of managers in specific areas of their responsibility for gaining commitment, eg performance management.

Developing ownership

A sense of belonging is enhanced if there is a feeling of 'ownership' among employees. Not just in the literal sense of owning shares (although this can help), but also in the sense of believing they are genuinely accepted by management as a key part of the organization. This concept of 'ownership' extends to participating in decisions on new developments and changes in working practices which affect the individuals concerned. They should be involved in making those decisions and feel that their ideas have been listened to and that they have contributed to the outcome. They will then be more likely to accept the decision or change because it is owned by them, rather than being imposed by management.

Developing a sense of excitement in the job

A sense of excitement in the job can be created by concentrating on the intrinsic motivating factors such as responsibility, achievement and recognition, and using these principles to govern the way in which jobs are designed. Excitement in the job is also created by the quality of leadership, and the willingness of managers and supervisors to recognize that they will obtain increased motivation and commitment if they pay continuous attention to the ways in which they delegate responsibility, and give their staff the scope to use their skills and abilities.

Performance management

A performance management system is based on agreements between managers and individuals on objectives, standards of performance and improvement plans. Performance is then managed and reviewed against these objectives.

This system can help to cascade corporate objectives and values throughout the organization, so that consistency is achieved at all levels. Discussions on individual objectives are carried out within the context of departmental, unit and, ultimately, organizational objectives. The expectations of individuals are thus defined in terms of their own job, which they can more readily grasp and act upon than if they were asked to support some remote and, to them, irrelevant overall objectives. But individual objectives can be described in ways which support the achievement of those defined for higher levels in the organization.

Reward management

Reward management systems can make it clear that individuals will be rewarded in accordance with the extent to which they achieve objectives *and* uphold corporate values. The reward system can thus be used to reinforce the messages delivered through other channels of communication.

THE ROLE OF THE HUMAN RESOURCE SPECIALIST IN INCREASING COMMITMENT

All the initiatives described above are clearly within the remit of the HR specialist, who will be responsible for advising on and complementing communication, education, training and involvement programmes, and will be expected to develop and administer performance and reward management systems.

Chapter 9

Flexibility

Flexibility is one of the key concepts of human resource management. Guest (1989a) named the achievement of flexibility as one of its four main policy goals.

THE NEED FOR FLEXIBILITY

The emphasis on increased flexibility has arisen for four reasons.

1   *The need to be competitive* – this focuses attention on the more efficient use of human resources.

2   *The need to be adaptive* – the organization has to be able to respond quickly to change and to the new demands constantly being made upon it in turbulent and highly competitive conditions.

3   *The impact of new technology* – this is changing skill requirements and working arrangements – for example, cellular manufacturing systems.

4   *New organization structures* – the emergence of what Mintzberg (1981) termed the 'adhocracy' – a more fluid form of organization in which complex innovation takes place and which requires a more flexible approach to structure, the definition of work roles and how roles interact.

Although competitive pressures and new technologies may generally indicate that greater structural and operating flexibility is required, the extent to which this applies in any one organization must depend entirely on its environment and its technology. A bureaucratic and less flexible approach might be appropriate in some circumstances; a much more flexible approach might be unavoidable in others. And there will always be a choice – depending on the situation – of what priorities should be given to the different types of flexibility.

FUNCTIONAL, NUMERICAL AND FINANCIAL FLEXIBILITY

It was suggested by Atkinson (1984) that there are three kinds of flexibility.

1   *Functional flexibility*, which is sought so that employees can be redeployed quickly and smoothly between activities and tasks. Functional flexibility may require *multi-skilling* – craft workers who possess and can apply a number of skills covering, for example, both mechanical and electrical engineering, or manufacturing and maintenance activities.

2   *Numerical flexibility*, which is sought so that the number of employees can be quickly and easily increased or decreased in line with even short-term changes in the level of demand for labour.

3   *Financial flexibility*, which provides for pay levels to reflect the state of supply and demand in the external labour market, and also operates flexible pay systems which facilitate either functional or numerical flexibility.

THE FLEXIBLE FIRM

It was also claimed by Atkinson that there is a growing trend for firms to seek all three kinds of flexibility by developing an entirely new organization structure. This results in the development of what he termed the 'flexible firm'.

The new structure in the flexible firm involves the break-up of the labour force into increasingly peripheral, and therefore numerically flexible, groups of workers clustered around a numerically stable core group, which will conduct the organization's key, firm-specific activities. At the core, the emphasis is on functional flexibility. Shifting to the periphery, numerical flexibility becomes more important. As the market grows, the periphery expands to take up slack; as growth slows, the periphery contracts. At the core, only tasks and responsibilities change; the workers here are insulated from medium-term fluctuations in the market, whereas those in the periphery are exposed to them.

It is an elegant and beguiling theory which has gained a lot of attention. But has it any validity? Pollert (1988) thinks not: 'Although superficially persuasive, the model rests on an uncertain basis of confused assumptions and unsatisfactory evidence'. The basis for this conclusion is Pollert's extensive research which showed that there was little evidence of the existence or creation of 'flexible firms' which have deliberately set up 'cores' and made more use of peripheral workers. Growth in the number of part-time or temporary workers does not appear to be a result of policy choices by would-be flexible firms. Two-thirds of the growth of part-time jobs in the private and public services can be explained simply by the general employment growth of these industries. And there is little evidence of a dramatic increase in subcontracting in the private sector.

More recent analysis by McGregor and Sproull (1991) into labour use strategies and the flexible firm found that a strategic approach to the employment of peripheral labour is relatively uncommon. The national survey commissioned by the Department of Employment, which was the basis for this analysis, revealed that the number of establishments employing peripheral labour predicting an increase in use was less than the number predicting a decline, a result which was particularly marked in the case of temporary workers. The reasons offered by establishments anticipating increased use were almost exclusively 'traditional' in nature. Only 2 per cent reported reasons for increased use which were clearly identified with a desire for greater labour flexibility. The number of peripheral workers may increase, but this is because industries currently using high proportions of this type of labour, such as service industries, are expected to become relatively more important in the economy in employment terms.

Research conducted by IDS (1986) and NEDO (1986) also cast doubts on the concept of functional flexibility and the spread of multi-skilling. IDS questioned whether multi-skilling is, in fact, as widely or universally desired as advocates of flexibility suggest:

> Companies have widely different aims. Competitive pressures vary between sectors. Skill requirements are dependent on widely different technologies. More skill, different skill, less skill, can all be legitimate objectives. Generalizations about moving towards a small, highly flexible workforce may fit one company and be contradicted by the pressure towards a quite different workforce in another.

And NEDO found that any changes in manning did not often represent qualitative breaks with previous manning practices within individual firms, nor did the changes to manning practices observed encompass major changes to existing company cultures.

The model of the flexible firm was an idea for its time. It was grasped by futurologists like Handy (1984) who, in *The Future of Work*, apocalyptically predicted that:

> jobs will be shorter, jobs will be more difficult, more dispersed and, in many cases, more precarious... the contractual organization is with us, is growing and is likely to grow faster.

Later, in *Age of Unreason* (1989), he predicted that the 'shamrock organization', with a core-periphery structure, would be the firm of the future.

However, a re-evaluation by Atkinson and Meager (1986) of their flexible firm model led them to conclude that, although there was plenty of evidence of change: 'the outcome was more likely to be marginal, *ad hoc* and tentative, rather than a purposeful and strategic thrust to achieve flexibility'. And Pollert's research and analysis led her to the following strongly worded conclusion:

At a methodological level, the fusing of description and prescription into futurological predictions rests on the weak foundations of unjustified meta-generalizations and one-dimensional determinism.

But the demise of the flexible firm model as a prescription for the future does not destroy the case for developing more flexible approaches to managing organizations where the environment and technology indicate that such a move is necessary and potentially beneficial. There is a choice of arrangements as described below.

FLEXIBILITY ARRANGEMENTS

Flexibility arrangements, as means of achieving the most efficient use of human resources, can take the following forms:

- contract-based – new forms of employment contracts;
- time-based – shift working and flexible hours;
- job-based – job-related flexibilities;
- skills-based – multi-skilling;
- organization-based – the use of contract workers and part-timers;
- pay-based – more flexible reward systems.

Contract-based flexibility

Contract-based flexibility refers to employee contracts which specify flexibility as a key aspect of terms and conditions. Job descriptions are written in terms which emphasize the overall purpose of the job and its principal accountabilities. These are broadly related to the achievement of corporate or departmental objectives. The job description does not specify in detail the duties to be carried out by the job holder and may contain a catch-all phrase such as 'accountable for the performance within the capability of the job holder of such other duties as are required to achieve the overall purpose of the job'. Contract-based flexibility is also achieved by employing contract workers who are required to work on any task or in any area appropriate to their range of skills.

Time-based flexibility

Time-based flexibility can be achieved by the use of flexible hours. The most familiar method is flexitime, in which employees can vary their daily hours of work on either side of the core-time when they have to be present, provided the longer-term required hours are completed. Time-based flexibility can be achieved in companies with marked seasonal fluctuations in labour requirements, such as photo-processing, by negotiating annual hours agreements. These specify the annual hours to be worked and paid for, but within that total they incorporate provisions for longer hours at peak periods and shorter hours during troughs.

Job-based flexibility (functional flexibility)

Job-based flexibility means that workers can be moved from task to task, and may be expected to use a wider range of skills within their capability. Firms may want to introduce this type of flexibility because they need to make the fullest use of their human resources, especially when they are using increasingly sophisticated equipment and systems which must be properly maintained if they are to produce at their optimum level.

Functional flexibility also means that where workloads in different parts of a factory fluctuate widely, people can be moved in quickly to handle the extra demands. At the Book Club Associates' distribution centre, for example, it was essential to have full flexibility between the 250 staff involved in the storage, packing and despatch areas because of the need to respond to large but predictable workload changes in these functions.

In the UK, the 1970s and 1980s saw the end of many of the old demarcation rules which had bedevilled flexibility in British industry. A typical union agreement (Nissan Motor) in the 1980s stipulated the following.

1 To ensure the fullest use of facilities and manpower, there will be complete flexibility and mobility of employees.

2 It is agreed that changes in technology, processes and practices will be introduced and that such changes will affect both productivity and manning levels.

3 To ensure such flexibility and change, employees will undertake training for all work as required by the company. All employees will train other employees as required.

These arrangements are fairly typical, especially in international firms setting up in green-field sites. Full functional flexibility is often associated with the harmonization of terms and conditions of employment so that all staff, both office and factory workers, are treated alike as far as benefits are concerned.

Skill-based flexibility (multi-skilling)

Functional flexibility is only possible when employees possess the range of skills required to perform different tasks, for example machine operators having the necessary skills not only to operate their machinery, but also to carry out basic maintenance and deal with minor faults and breakdowns.

At Hardy Spicer in the 1980s a form of 'just-in-time' manufacture was introduced which included an integrated flexible flow line of dedicated CNC (computer numerical control) machine cells, linked by a robotized pallet convey or system and programmable controls. This type of manufacturing system pointed to the need for multi-skilling in which 'system technicians' on the production line had to have a range of skills, including machine set up and basic maintenance, as well as taking responsibility for loading, quality and output. These technicians had to have a wide understanding of tool gauging, hydraulics, electrics and basic electronics. A 20-week training programme was required.

Multi-skilling is about developing the capacities of people to undertake a wider range of tasks and to exercise greater responsibility. It is therefore consistent with that aspect of HRM philosophy which emphasizes the importance of investing in people and, therefore, of human resource development. Multi-skilling, however, makes considerable demands on the organization to provide the training required and to motivate people to learn.

Multi-skilling, according to Cross (1991), is based on two principles. The first is competency within the workplace, ie the ability of a single individual to assess and rectify problems as they occur day by day, regardless of the nature of the problem. The second is the full utilization of capabilities, ie the only limitation on who does what, how and when, are the skills that an individual has or can acquire, the time available to perform any new or additional tasks and the requirements of safety.

It is necessary to set clear objectives for the levels of benefits expected from multi-skilling, including better use of resources, focusing attention on critical success factors and increased productivity. It is also essential to decide how the success of multi-skilling can be measured and introduce methods of monitoring progress.

At Shell's Stanlow plant in the UK a productivity/flexibility deal was negotiated with the union in 1985 which provided for multi-skilling. The progress made in implementing the deal was monitored under the following headings.

- *Attitudes to the deal* – how positive?
- *Operating* – how efficient?
- *Service to operations* – how effective?
- *Training* – how effective?
- *Representation* – are the new representative systems working well?
- *Consultation* – are the existing and new consultation structures working well?
- *Contractors* – how were they being used? Are their numbers reducing?
- *Overtime* – how well is it being controlled?
- *Costs* – are targets for cost reduction being achieved?

Organization-based flexibility

Organization-based approaches to flexibility include making more use of part-time and temporary staff or contract workers. Although the evidence as mentioned above does not indicate that this route is being followed to any great extent, there is still scope in some situations, especially the service industries, to develop a strategy for relying on a smaller nucleus of permanent employees, the so-called core.

Pay-based flexibility

Reward policies should allow for flexibility in operating the reward system in response to business fluctuations, the rapidly changing pressures to which the organization and its employees are likely to be subjected, the demand for different types of skills and variations in market rates for different categories of staff.

Flexibility can be achieved by:

- increasing the proportion of variable performance-related pay in the total package;
- avoiding the use of rigid, hierarchical pay structures by such means as the use of pay curves, where progression is dependent on competence and performance;
- introducing skill-based pay systems to reward employees who acquire extra skills;
- not having a mechanistic system of relating rewards to performance;
- relating pay awards entirely to merit and increases in market rates, thus avoiding a separate and explicit link with increases in the cost of living, and giving scope to award good performers more and poor performers less;
- allowing employees greater choice in the benefits they receive;
- recognizing that the organization must respond quickly to the problems caused by skill shortages and market rate pressures, and flexing the pay arrangements accordingly.

FLEXIBILITY AND THE HR SPECIALIST

The areas in which the HR specialist can advise on the scope for increasing flexibility and help in developing it are as follows.

- *Contracts of employment and job descriptions* – introducing more flexible contracts and less restrictive job descriptions.
- *Working hours* – designing, negotiating and implementing flexible hours systems.
- *Job and work design* – enlarging and enriching the range of responsibilities of individuals and teams.
- *Flexibility agreements* – negotiating agreements with trade unions and monitoring their implementation.
- *Training* – providing training both to enhance and to broaden skills.

- *Resourcing* – seeking ways of using part-time, temporary or contract workers where this is appropriate.
- *Pay* – developing flexible reward systems.

Chapter 10

Teamworking

THE SIGNIFICANCE OF TEAMWORKING

HRM is largely about making the best use of people. Although HRM policies and practices often focus on the individual it has to be recognized that organizations are cooperative systems which consist of groups of people working together. They may be working in formal groups set up to achieve a defined purpose or they may be working informally.

Teamworking becomes more significant when the technology or operating processes require 'cellular' working or considerable interaction between people carrying out different functions, but with a common purpose. Effective teamworking is more important during periods of rapid change or crisis. An organization which has to adapt quickly to its changing competitive, economic or social environment will rely upon good teamwork so that it can pool resources and respond fast to the new opportunities or threats.

The top management team in a responsive and adaptive organization will often operate on a collegiate basis. Each director may be concerned with a particular function or discipline, but they share responsibility for results, and get involved jointly and severally to deal with issues. Informal sub-groups or task forces are created, when necessary, which cut across functional boundaries and address a common task. The leader of the top management team – the chief executive officer – will join in the task forces on equal terms. Leadership may indeed be assumed by any member of the team who has the special skills required to deal with the situation.

The tendency for organizations to become flatter as layers of management or supervision are stripped out creates the need for better teamwork. In these circumstances managers will have larger spans of control and will have to delegate more responsibility to their teams, who will be forced to coordinate their own work rather than rely upon their boss to do it for them. In this type of organization interdisciplinary project teams become more important. The instant availability of management information and the communication facilities provided by information technology assist informal teams to operate more efficiently.

At office or shop floor level autonomous work groups may be set up which are responsible for all aspects of their operation and may not have an appointed leader.

HRM policies should be designed to promote effective teamwork in the situations described above. This chapter examines how such policies can be developed and applied under the following headings:

- team processes;
- team development;
- team effectiveness;
- team roles;
- approach to achieving good teamwork;
- teamworking in action;
- introducing teamworking;
- teambuilding and interactive skills training.

TEAM PROCESSES

Task and maintenance functions

The following functions need to be carried out in teams:

- *task* – initiating, information seeking, diagnosing, opinion seeking, evaluating, decision making;
- *maintenance* – encouraging, compromising, peace-keeping, clarifying, summarizing, standard setting.

It is the job of the team leader or leaders to ensure that these functions operate effectively. Leaderless teams can work, but only in special circumstances. A leader is almost essential – whether official or self-appointed. The style adopted by the leader affects the way the team operates. If he or she is respected, this will increase the group's cohesiveness and its ability to get things done. An inappropriately authoritarian style creates tension and resentment. An over-permissive style means that respect for the leader diminishes and the team will not function so effectively.

Group ideology and cohesion

In the course of interacting and carrying out its task and maintenance functions, a group develops an ideology which affects the attitudes and actions of its members, and the degree of satisfaction which they feel.

If the group ideology is strong and individual members identify closely with the group, it will become increasingly cohesive. Group norms or implicit rules will be evolved which define what is acceptable behaviour and what is not. The impact of group cohesion can, however, result in negative as well as positive results. Janis's (1972) study of the decision making of US foreign policy groups established that a cohesive group of individuals, sharing a common fate, exerts a strong pressure towards conformity. He coined the term 'group think' to describe the exaggeration of irrational tendencies which appears to occur in groups. He argued that a group setting can magnify weakness of judgement. To be 'one of us' is not always a good thing in management (or political) circles. A sturdy spirit of independence, even a maverick tendency, may be more conducive to correct decision making. Although teamworking is a good thing, so is flexibility. These need not be incompatible, but could be if there is too much emphasis on cohesion and loyalty to the team.

Identification

Individuals will identify with their team if they like the other members, approve of the purpose and work of the team, and wish to be associated with the standing of the group in the organization. Identification will be more complex if the standing of the team is good.

TEAM DEVELOPMENT

Tuckman (1965) identified four stages of team development.

1 *Forming*, when there is anxiety, dependence on the leader and testing to find out the nature of the situation and the task, and what behaviour is acceptable.

2 *Storming*, where there is conflict, emotional resistance to the demands of the task, resistance to control and even rebellion against the leader.

3 *Norming*, when group cohesion is developed, norms emerge, views are exchanged openly, mutual support and cooperation increase and the group acquires a sense of its identity.

4 *Performing*, when interpersonal problems are resolved, roles are flexible and functional, there are constructive attempts to complete tasks and energy is available for effective work.

TEAM EFFECTIVENESS

An effective team is likely to be one in which the structure, leadership and methods of operation are relevant to the requirements of the task. The Longwall and Ahmedabad studies carried out by the Tavistock Institute – Trist (1963) and Miller and Rice (1967) – emphasized the importance of commitment to the whole group task and the need to group people in a way which ensures that they are related to each other by way of the requirements of task performance and task interdependence.

In an effective team its purpose is clear and its members feel the task is important, both to them and to the organization (the concept of saliency). According to McGregor (1960), the main features of a well-functioning, creative team are as follows.

1   The atmosphere tends to be informal, comfortable and relaxed.

2   There is a lot of discussion in which everyone participates initially, but it remains pertinent to the task of the group.

3   The task or objective of the team is well understood and accepted by the members. There will have been free discussion of the objective at some point, until it was formulated in such a way that the members of the team could commit themselves to it.

4   The members listen to each other. Every idea is given a hearing. People do not appear to be afraid of being considered foolish by putting forth a creative thought, even if it seems fairly extreme.

5   There is disagreement. Disagreements are not suppressed or overridden by premature team action. The reasons are carefully examined, and the team seeks to resolve them rather than to dominate the dissenter.

6   Most decisions are reached by consensus in which it is clear that everybody is in general agreement and willing to go along. Formal voting is at a minimum; the team does not accept a simple majority as a proper basis for action.

7   Criticism is frequent, frank and relatively comfortable. There is little evidence of personal attack, either openly or in a hidden fashion.

8   People are free in expressing their feelings as well as their ideas, both on the problem and on the group's operation.

9   When action is taken, clear assignments are made and accepted.

10   The leader of the team does not dominate it, nor does the team defer unduly to him or her. There is little evidence of a struggle for power as the team operates. The issue is not who controls, but how to get the job done.

These characteristics together present an ideal which might be striven for but is seldom attained. The extent to which it is possible or even desirable for them to be achieved depends on the situation. A mechanistic or bureaucratic type of enterprise – where this is appropriate to the technology – cannot allow its formal organizational units to function just like this, although it should try to ensure that any committees, task forces or project teams which are set up do exhibit these forms of behaviour.

TEAM ROLES

Bales (1956) found that effective teams need people who help to get things done. They also need people who are concerned with the social side of working in a group. Task-oriented team members are most influential, but socially inclined members are most liked.

Belbin (1981) identified eight different roles played by management team members.

1 *Chairpersons* – control the way in which a team moves towards the group objectives by making the best use of team resources; recognizing where the team's strengths and weaknesses lie and ensuring the best use is made of each team member's role.

2 *Shapers* – specify the ways in which team effort is applied, directing attention generally to the setting of objectives and priorities, and seeking to impose some shape or pattern on group discussion and on the outcome of group activities.

3 *Company workers* – turn concepts and plans into practical working procedures and carry out agreed plans systematically and efficiently.

4 *Plants* – specify new ideas and strategies, with special attention to major issues. Look for possible breaks in approaches to the problems with which the group is confronted.

5 *Resource investigators* – explore and report on ideas, developments and resources outside the group, creating external contacts which might be useful to the team and conducting any subsequent negotiations.

6 *Monitor–evaluators* – analyze problems and evaluate ideas and suggestions so that the team is better placed to take better decisions.

7 *Teamworkers* – support members in their strengths (ie building on their suggestions), underpin members in their shortcomings, improve communications between members and foster team spirit generously.

8 *Completer–finishers* – ensure that the team is protected from mistakes, actively search for work which needs more than a usual degree of attention, and maintain a sense of urgency in the team.

Belbin suggests that, although the main roles of team members can be slotted into one or other of these categories, most people have an alternative, back-up role which they use as necessary.

APPROACHES TO ACHIEVING GOOD TEAMWORK

Walton (1985a) has commented that in the new commitment-based organization it will often be teams rather than individuals who will be the organizational units accountable for performance.

However, teamwork, as Wickens (1987) has said, 'is not dependent on people working in groups but upon everyone working towards the same objectives'. The Nissan concept of teamwork, as quoted by Wickens, is expressed in its general principles and emphasizes the need to:

■ promote mutual trust and cooperation between the company, its employees and the union;
■ recognize that all employees, at whatever level, have a valued part to play in the success of the company;
■ seek actively the contributions of all employees in furthering these goals.

Waterman (1988) has noted that teamwork:

is a tricky business; it requires people to pull together toward a set of shared goals or values. It does not mean that they always agree on the best way to get there. When they don't agree they should discuss, even argue these differences.

Pascale (1990) underlined this point when he wrote that successful companies can use conflict to stay ahead: 'We are almost always better served when conflict is surfaced and channelled, not suppressed.' The pursuit of teamwork should not lead to a 'bland' climate in the organization in which nothing new or challenging ever happens. It is all very well to be 'one big happy family', but this could be disastrous if it breeds complacency and a cosy feeling that the family spirit comes first, whatever is happening in the outside world.

Things to do to improve teamwork

■ Pick people who will fit the culture and work well with others, but who are still capable of taking their own line when necessary.
■ Keep on emphasizing that constructive teamwork is a key core value in the organization.
■ Set overlapping or interlocking objectives for people who have to work together. These will take the form of targets to be achieved or projects to be completed by joint action.
■ Assess people's performance, not only on the results they achieve, but also on the degree to which they uphold the value of teamwork.
■ Encourage people to build networks – things get done in organizations, as in the outside world, on the basis of who you know as well as what you know. It is no good being right if you cannot carry other people along with you. And this is best done through informal channels rather than relying on reports, memoranda or committees. This, incidentally, is an approach which people without a strong power base in the organization, such as some personnel managers, can use to good effect.
■ Set up interdepartmental project teams with a brief to get on with it.
■ Clamp down on unproductive politics.

- Describe and think of the organization as a system of interlocking teams united by a common purpose. Don't emphasize hierarchies. Abolish departmental boundaries if they are getting in the way, but do not be alarmed if there is disagreement – remember the value of *constructive* conflict.
- Devise and implement commitment and communications strategies which develop mutuality and identification.
- Hold 'away days' and conferences for work teams so they can get together and explore some of the real issues without the pressures of their day-to-day jobs.
- Recognize and reward people who have worked well in teams.
- Introduce team bonus systems – rewarding teams for achieving targets.
- Use training programmes to build relationships. This can often be a far more beneficial result of a training course than the increase in skills or knowledge which was its ostensible purpose.
- Use teambuilding and interactive skills training to supplement the other approaches. But do not rely upon them to have any effect, unless the messages they convey are in line with the organization's culture and values.

TEAMWORKING IN ACTION

Teamworking can take place in autonomous working groups using 'high performance work design' techniques. It is particularly important to develop teams in cell-based working systems.

Autonomous working groups

An autonomous work group is allocated an overall task and given discretion over how the work is done. This provides for intrinsic motivation by giving people autonomy and the means to control their work, which will include feedback information.

The conceptual basis of the autonomous work group approach is socio-technical systems theory, which suggests that the best results are obtained if grouping is such that workers are primarily related to each other by way of task performance and task interdependence. As Emery (1980) has stated:

In designing a social system efficiently to operate capital intensive plant the key problem is that of creating self-managing groups to man the interface with technical system.

An autonomous work group may:

- enlarge individual jobs to include a wider range of operative skills;

- decide on methods of work and the planning, scheduling and control of work;
- distribute tasks itself among its members;
- exercise quality control over its work.

High performance work design

High performance work design is an approach to job design aimed at maximizing the effectiveness of teams, especially in high-technology manufacturing systems. As described by Buchanan (1987), it has the following characteristics.

1 Management clearly defines what it needs in the form of new technology or methods of production and the results expected from its introduction.

2 Multi-skilling is encouraged – that is, job demarcation lines are eliminated as far as possible, and encouragement and training are provided for employees to acquire new skills.

3 Equipment is selected which can be used flexibly and is laid out to allow freedom of movement.

4 Autonomous working groups are established, each with around a dozen members, and with full 'back-to-back' responsibility for product assembly and testing, fault-finding and some maintenance.

5 Managers adopt a supportive rather than an autocratic style with teams and team leaders (this is the most difficult part of the system to introduce).

6 Support systems are provided for kit-marshalling and material supply, which help the teams to function effectively as productive units.

7 Management sets goals and standards for success.

8 The new system is introduced with great care by means of involvement and communication programmes.

9 Thorough training is carried out on the basis of an assessment of training needs.

10 The payment system is specially designed with staff participation to fit their needs, as well as those of management.

Cell-based working – a case history

Digital Equipment Corporation's very large scale integration (VLSI) operation assembles and tests semiconductors for use in Digital's range of business computers. As reported by IRS (1990), when the assembly unit was established in 1987 the unit's management decided that the operation's structure needed to be changed. The reasons for this decision included:

- rapid developments in semiconductor technology which meant that the assembly process could double in complexity with each new product;
- a desire to reduce the wastage rate, since each silicon wafer has already completed 100 key process steps by the time it reaches the assembly stage and mistakes cannot be rectified;
- the recognition that operators had skills and abilities which were not being exploited in a 'mechanistic serial process'; and
- the emphasis in the Digital corporate philosophy on 'quality of working life' and development of the individual employee.

Other factors taken into account were the needs to cut down cycle time, to turn orders round in a shorter period and to build in flexibility so that small batches of different types of product could be processed quickly. However, greatly increased productivity was not a priority.

The plan for change

The new operational strategy, designed to 'build intelligence' into the assembly process, was devised by seven assembly staff managers at the beginning of 1987. They proposed to:

- 'vertically integrate' the process, regrouping machines in product lines, so that each line would have responsibility for the construction of a component from start to finish with as few joins as possible;
- divide sections of the new lines into workcells with maintenance and quality control conducted within the cell;
- train operators to be proficient in all the production stages in their cell and give them an understanding of the complete assembly process; and
- introduce just-in-time (JIT) working which eliminates the build-up of stock throughout the production process and cuts inventory costs.

At the beginning of the reorganization employees received a commitment that there would be no redundancies as a result of the programme.

Setting up the cells

The formation of the workcells and the teams in them was made in the first place following the reorganization by management of the assembly layout. Previously, machines had been grouped according to production stage so that all those operating one type of machine worked in proximity on batches of circuits passed on from the stage before. The reorganized lines have one of each machine per line arranged in the sequence of actual production so that a product passes directly down the line and any faults detected at the test stage can be traced back to a single machine.

The cells were created by artificially grouping together certain steps in the line. The first layout devised by management gave each line six cells. However, within two months employees on the line requested that some cells be merged and now there are five cells and cell teams per line of 25 employees.

Training for teamwork

Accompanying the shift to a cell-based production line was the introduction of the concept of teamworking. This was intended to help the members of a cell to take collective responsibility for quality and process control within their area and to work together to solve any operational problems. In the middle of 1988, for a period of two months only, two of the three shifts worked on the line in any 24 hours while the third received training in teamworking and the operation of JIT and quality control.

Team training included a course on basic problem-solving techniques developed by Digital's corporate quality section, which teaches the use of statistical process control, and Pareto and fishbone diagrams. Some cell members were also taught how to improve the presentation of ideas to a group and how to hold effective meetings. Since this initial training phase for all operators, team-related training (such as courses in chairing meetings) has been arranged for representatives of each cell as part of the skills training programme.

Team responsibilities

Although they were trained in group working and problem solving, the line teams were initially given few responsibilities beyond those of quality and stock control. However, during the next two and a half years many responsibilities were devolved to the operators. Any changes to layout or organization, which do not have an impact outside the cell, may be made by a simple majority of team members. Changes affecting other cells are taken to the shift team (made up of leading hands and supervisors) for discussion. Cell teams are responsible for recording their own output, cycle times, reject levels and productivity on notice boards placed beside the line.

Each team has to budget its time three months in advance, taking into account its training commitments and production targets and, if the two cannot be matched, then the team puts in a request for overtime.

Success

The overall success of the adoption of teamworking, just-in-time and quality management is demonstrated by a number of measures. Through JIT the number of circuits in the system at any time for an output of 30,000 per week has dropped from 45,000 to around 12,000. The minimum batch size which the line can produce has been reduced from 300 to 90 and is expected to drop to 50. This allows small orders from other Digital companies to be filled without a build-up of surplus stock.

As a result of the quality programme the yield of circuits with no fault has risen from 92 per cent in the middle of 1988 to 97.8 per cent in the middle of 1990, compared with an average improvement across the industry of 0.02 per cent in the same two years. In the same period the cycle time has been reduced from 10 days to 2.1 days, the speed at which the company could previously produce only occasional rush orders.

Despite considerable upheaval and a radical change in working practices, VLSI has maintained a rate of labour turnover of less than 2 per cent a year since the restructuring.

INTRODUCING TEAMWORKING

A report by NEDO (1991) on introducing teamworking in the clothing industry stated that the main motive in most of the companies visited during the research was to improve response times, which were cut from six weeks under the previous assembly line system to around a week or less. Best-selling lines can be more readily pursued – a real gain in the fashion business – and costly levels of work in progress and stocks of finished goods reduced. These savings, however, are usually offset by increased wage costs.

But there are gains on the labour cost side too. In most companies, the number of supervisors had dropped by 20–30 per cent; teams are encouraged to manage themselves and to control the flow of work between members. Because team members pass work to each other, each acts as the quality inspector for previous members, fewer people are needed in quality control and the number of 'seconds' falls substantially; some firms have abolished quality control departments. In many cases, labour turnover and absenteeism have fallen significantly.

Developing team working: a seven-stage plan

The NEDO research therefore showed that teamworking can have substantial benefits. But, as Cannel (1992) notes, its introduction needs to be properly handled: there are several examples of failure, apparently because managements have rushed into change without sufficient forethought. Planning is essential, and the following paragraphs consider the stages necessary if teamworking is to be introduced successfully. What follows is based on the experience of garment manufacturers, but the stages should be similar in other sectors.

Stage 1: Initial preparation

Senior people in the company need to consider the reasons for introducing teamwork – for example, is it primarily to improve response times, or is reducing labour turnover and absenteeism just as important? Is it vital to have a potential throughput time of a day or less, or will a few days suffice? Is the extra cost, which is almost certainly involved in ultra-quick response, worth it?

Stage 2: Project planning

The American companies visited had one dedicated individual, or a team of managers, with the task of developing the project. They believed that if the job were given to someone with heavy day-to-day responsibilities, that person would be unlikely to give it the time it deserved, and the outcome could be failure. The individual or team needs to know that the project has the full support of senior people over the medium and long term, and that it is not simply seen as a 'quick fix'. If a team is formed, it should include people from various disciplines; engineering, work study and personnel, for example.

Stage 3: Develop plans

The individual or team responsible will need to develop ideas, which takes time and requires careful and formal planning. For example, the formation and composition of teams, training, pay systems, and the size and physical layout of groups need to be considered. Pre-production planning, which assumes greater importance because of the reduction of buffer stocks, also needs to be revised. Time should also be taken to develop consensus, particularly among middle managers and supervisors, who may feel that their authority is threatened. American experience suggests that six months from beginning planning to establishing the first group is reasonable.

Stage 4: Communication

If a trade union is recognized, the relevant full-time official and shop stewards should be consulted as soon as possible, and certainly well before the announcement to the workforce generally. If their support can be gained, it will help to sell the concept more widely and, of course, such consultation should continue at every subsequent stage.

After the planning stage, everyone will have to be told what is proposed. How the announcement is made will, to some extent, depend on the size of plant and what shift systems, if any, are operated. Making the announcement to a meeting of everyone in the factory has the advantage that they will all receive the same message, but a considerable disadvantage is that, in a large meeting, many people will feel unable to ask questions. The best way may be a combination of the factory-wide meeting, at which the announcement should be made by the chairperson or managing director to establish the commitment of senior people, followed by meetings of groups of around 20, involving the factory manager and project leader, at which there can be questions and discussion.

Whatever the manner of the announcement, the policy should be one of openness and honesty, and undue expectations should not be raised by promising too much too soon. The reasons for the proposed change need to be described (eg to increase speed of response, to improve quality). The advantages from the point of view of the workforce (eg more stable earnings, a more varied job); and the transitional arrangements (in particular, training) should also be spelled out. The briefing should be supported with simple written material, perhaps in question and answer form.

Stage 5: Training

Virtually all the interviewees said that they wished they had carried out more training. In the USA, teamworking experiments have failed because of insufficient attention to training, which should have the following elements.

The first is managerial and supervisory training, which should take place before the first teams are established. American practitioners recommend at least ten two-hour training sessions over two or three weeks. Subjects could include teambuilding, communications, problem solving, motivation, quality and participative management.

The second element is operative training, which falls into three areas.

1 *Team working and related skills.* This had clearly been difficult for the companies visited. With teamworking, operatives need to communicate with each other more than previously and to establish consensus. One very American method is to get *all* team members to agree on a name for the team at an early stage. This, in itself, forces communication, and the very process of coming to agreement can be used to draw lessons about cooperation and communication. Problem-solving exercises can also be used.

2 *Technical issues.* Team members also need to know something about machine maintenance, quality, line balancing and what one interviewee called 'the relationship between time and money'. Here the practical approach – giving people stop-watches and calculators, and letting them work out real problems for themselves – may be more effective than theoretical training. Such training might be carried out before a group is actually set up early in its life. Supervisors might participate with teams in such training, to reinforce their changed role.

3 *Multi-skilling.* The firms visited believed that each team member should be able to carry out, say, three operations. Ultimately every

team member should be able to do every job within the group. This has the additional advantage of enabling the group to cover for absence without using 'floaters'. Multi-skilling can be achieved by conventional training, but it can also be achieved by one team member with a particular skill training perhaps two of his or her colleagues in it. This also helps to raise the self-esteem of the individual doing the training, and to develop team communication and cohesiveness.

Stage 6: Developing pilot teams

The companies visited had formed one or two teams initially, and then added new teams after six months or so. This gradualist approach enabled experiments (and mistakes) to be made. In the USA, the initial teams had mainly been formed from volunteers. This may be preferable to compulsion, which can give the wrong message, and there is some truth in the old saying about the value of volunteers as against pressed men. Against this, there may come a point when the supply of volunteers will dry up, and to ensure that all teams are reasonably balanced it may be best to co-opt people from the start. This has generally been the course followed by British clothing companies.

The first team or teams should be formed from people whose performance, attendance and other attributes are around average, so that a fair assessment of the benefits and difficulties can be made. The management chooses people on the basis of their skills, the number of jobs they can do, similar efficiencies and capacities, attitude, attendance records and personal compatibility, in order to produce a balanced team. Selecting people with poor attendance records or abrasive attitudes may be demoralizing to the rest of the team even before it fully exists, and before the beneficial effects of peer pressure begin to work. Interviewing each potential member individually to explain the concepts further and to clear up any misapprehensions should help to secure commitment.

Stage 7: Forming further teams

After the pilot schemes have been in operation for a few months, management will need to ask what has been learned from them, what should be kept and what should be changed. If it is decided to convert the whole factory, low and high performers will need special consideration. In some companies, low performers have been difficult to place because of resistance from potential team colleagues; the solution has been to shift them to preparation areas or to form a low performing group.

High performers can also pose problems. Wide earnings disparities can be detrimental to building team attitudes, since high earners used to individual piece rates may resist giving up some of their pay to lower performers if payment is on a group basis. The converse, however, is that in some cases high performers have pulled others up to previously unattained levels. Some companies have red-circled high performers' earnings so that their pay is maintained until it is subsumed in general pay increases.

Chapter 11

HRM and Total Quality Management

HRM AND QUALITY

Quality, which in essence means customer satisfaction, is generally recognized today as the key to the achievement of competitive advantage. Innovation and cost reduction are still important but they are to no avail if, ultimately, customers reject the product because it does not meet their expectations.

Quality is achieved through people and, in accordance with a basic HRM principle, investment in people is a prerequisite for achieving high quality standards.

TOTAL QUALITY

Total quality can be defined as a systematic way of guaranteeing that all activities within an organization happen the way they have been planned in order to meet the defined needs and requirements of customers and clients. In other words, it is designed to match internal systems to external requirements.

Key features of total quality include:

- commitment from top management to provide visible leadership to the whole approach;
- an objective of customer satisfaction, both internal and external, at all levels within an organization;
- continuous improvement creating an environment where each individual is committed to seeking ways of enhancing performance;
- measurement on a regular basis to ensure a clear focus on facts and data so that necessary improvements may be made.

In short, as Collard (1992) has indicated, total quality is a way of life within an organization. It reflects the culture of that organization and therefore is dependent entirely on the commitment and actions of the individuals within the organization. Total quality is based on a philosophy of 'success through people', which means putting people at the heart of the process.

TOTAL QUALITY MANAGEMENT
What it is

Total quality management is an intensive, long-term effort directed at the creation and maintenance of the high standards of product quality and services expected by customers. The object is significantly to increase the awareness of all employees that quality is vital to the organization's success and their future. The business must be transformed into a unit which exists to deliver value to customers by satisfying their needs. The steps to successful total quality management (TQM) are the following:

- measure quality;
- determine the cost of quality;
- incorporate quality objectives into strategic plans;
- build TQM into accountabilities of every job and into all related systems (eg performance appraisal);
- form quality teams which are integrated, top to bottom and bottom to top, as well as laterally to include suppliers and customers;
- obtain demonstrable commitment from top management;
- recognize and reward quality improvement.

What it isn't

Total quality management is not a 'programme', a term which implies a finite beginning and end. It is, in fact, a continuous performance.

However, although the emphasis on quality can never be relaxed, quality management is not simply a matter of demanding ever-increasing quality target levels, thus implying that acceptable quality is unattainable. This is a defeatist approach. Neither is it a matter of using quality control and inspection systems, and expecting that these alone will improve quality, although they have their uses as monitoring and measuring devices. Total quality is not achieved by techniques such as quality circles, which, as Wickens (1987) says, are no more than 'a fine tuning mechanism for companies whose quality is already good'.

Quality is an attitude of mind which leads to appropriate behaviours and actions. It has to be, as at Nissan, 'the centrepiece of the company's philosophy, with commitment *at every level* to a zero-defect product' (author's emphasis).

Quality assurance and BS 5750

BS 5750 provides the national standards which tell suppliers and manufacturers what is required of a quality system. It sets out how an organization can establish, document and maintain an effective quality system which will demonstrate to customers that the organization is committed to quality and is able to meet their quality needs. It therefore provides for quality assurance standards, but these are not ends in themselves. They are only a basis for a total quality management (TQM) approach, as described above.

The approach to TQM

Giles and Williams (1991) have suggested that quality management should be achieved by the application of basic principles of motivation throughout the organization:

> Top management sets the priorities and initial goals and allocates responsibility. Those made responsible then say what they need in the way of resources and top management back-up to achieve these. The process continues down through the hierarchy until all those on the shop floor have negotiated what their priorities are and the resources needed to achieve these. Goals are thus set in such a way that everyone's work fits in with the organization's priorities and each person knows what they have to do, in measurable terms.

Collard (1989) suggests: 'Quality improvement should always be at the forefront of *everything* that is done, continuously reinforced and developed by management through the systems, processes and organizations which make each improvement possible.'

TQM AND THE HR SPECIALIST

The HR function should play a key role in total quality management at the strategic, operational and process levels.

Strategic contribution

At the strategic level the HR specialist can advise on the culture and climate of the organization and its readiness to change in the direction of a quality approach to all aspects of the business. The HR function can also contribute by advising on the skill base required for TQM and how these skills can be developed. Finally, and importantly, the function can promote the more effective use of the communication system to get the quality message across.

Operational contribution

At the operational level, the human resource function can play a major part in the education and training programmes which are at the heart of the development of TQM. These will include training in quality awareness, approaches to achieving quality, problem and fault correction techniques, teamworking and the acquisition of new skills as part of a multi-skilling process. As Collard (1992) says, 'total quality provides an opportunity for using training and development as the engine room for change and the heart of the total quality programme'.

Process contribution

The HR specialist can help a TQM initiative to succeed by designing support systems in the following areas.

- *Reward management* – ensuring that quality and teamworking to achieve quality are rewarded, as well as hitting output or sales targets.
- *Performance management* – providing for values such as quality and customer service to be key factors in setting objectives and reviewing performance.
- *Skills provision* – ensuring that recruitment, development and training processes reflect the likely new needs for skill required in a total quality management system.
- *Management development* – emphasizing the need for continuous improvement and learning in the management and career development process.

Part IV

HRM in Action

Chapter 12

Resourcing

HRM AND RESOURCING

HRM is fundamentally about matching human resources to the strategic and operational needs of the organization, and ensuring the full utilization of those resources. It is concerned not only with obtaining and keeping the number and quality of staff required, but also with selecting and promoting people who 'fit' the culture and the strategic requirements of the organization.

The aim of HRM resourcing policies, as expressed by Keep (1989), is:

> To obtain the right basic material in the form of a workforce endowed with the appropriate qualities, skills, knowledge and potential for future training. The selection and recruitment of workers best suited to meeting the needs of the organization ought to form a core activity upon which most other HRM policies geared towards development and motivation could be built.

HRM places more emphasis than conventional personnel management on finding people whose attitudes and behaviour are likely to be congruent with what management believes to be appropriate and conducive to success. In the words of Townley (1989) organizations are concentrating more on 'the attitudinal and behavioural characteristics of employees'. This tendency has its dangers. Innovative and adaptive organizations need non-conformists, even mavericks, who can 'buck the system'. If managers recruit people 'in their own image' there is the risk of staffing the organization with conformist clones and of perpetuating a dysfunctional culture – one which may have been successful in the past, but is no longer appropriate (nothing fails like success).

The HRM approach to resourcing therefore emphasizes that matching resources to organizational requirements does not simply mean maintaining the status quo and perpetuating a moribund culture. It can, and often does, mean radical changes in thinking about the competences required in the future to achieve sustainable growth and cultural change. HRM resourcing policies address two fundamental questions.

1   What kind of people do we need to compete effectively, now and in the foreseeable future?

2   What do we have to do to attract, develop and keep these people?

Integrating business and resourcing strategies

The philosophy behind the HRM approach to resourcing is that it is people who implement the strategic plan. As Quinn Mills (1985) has put it, the process is one of 'planning with people in mind'.

The integration of business and resourcing strategies is based on an understanding of the direction in which the organization is going and of the resulting human resource needs in terms of:

- numbers required in relation to projected activity levels;
- skills required on the basis of technological and product–market developments and strategies to enhance quality or reduce costs;
- the impact of organizational restructuring as a result of rationalization, decentralization, delayering, mergers, product or market development, or the introduction of new technology – for example, cellular manufacturing;
- plans for changing the culture of the organization in such areas as ability to deliver, performance standards, quality, customer service, teamworking and flexibility which indicate the need for people with different attitudes, beliefs and personal characteristics.

These factors will be strongly influenced by the type of business strategies adopted by the organization and the sort of business it is in. These may be expressed in such terms as the Boston Consulting Group's classification of businesses as 'wild cat, star, cash cow or dog'; or Miles and Snow's (1978 and 1984) typology of 'defender, prospector and analyzer' organizations (see also page 144).

Resourcing strategies exist to provide the people and skills required to support the business strategy, but they should also contribute to the formulation of that strategy. HR directors have an obligation to point out to their colleagues the human resource opportunities and constraints which will affect the achievement of strategic plans. In mergers or acquisitions, for example, the ability of management within the company to handle the new situation and the quality of management in the new business will be important considerations.

Resourcing activities

Implementing an HRM resourcing strategy involves the following activities:

- identifying and analyzing the organization's requirements for people and skills (the demand side);

- assessing the present and future availability of people from the various internal and external labour markets (the supply side);

- planning and implementing recruitment campaigns;

- extending and enhancing skills through training;

- managing upward mobility within the internal labour market in terms of promotion or upgrading and skills development;

- seeking alternative and more cost-effective methods of satisfying needs;

- managing the retention of people.

This chapter concentrates on the activities related to demand and supply forecasting, preparing the resourcing plan, methods of improving selection in an HRM context, alternative sources of labour and retention strategies.

DEMAND AND SUPPLY CONSIDERATIONS

Demand and supply considerations are handled by assessing human resource requirements as indicated by strategic and shorter-term plans, analyzing stocks and flows in the internal labour market and analyzing the various external markets.

Human resource requirements

Strategic and shorter-term business plans should provide information on plans and proposals for:

- new ventures;
- opening up new markets;
- introducing new products or services;
- creating new activities or functions;
- introducing new technology – operational and information;
- disinvestments;
- reducing the size of existing activities;
- merging or transferring activities;
- decentralization;
- organizational restructuring, eg delayering or eliminating regional or district offices;
- cost reduction;
- productivity improvements.

These plans can be translated into shorter-term forecasts of activity levels, and manpower budgets. The latter will indicate the numbers required by unit, department, function and skill. The plans will also indicate any specific actions which will be necessary to deal with likely requirements for additional staff or the need to reduce the number of employees (downsizing).

The strategic and business plans should define the quantity of people needed, and also skills requirements, so that steps can be taken to satisfy them by recruitment and training activities.

Stocks and flows analysis

The analysis of stocks and flows defines the internal labour market – how people move into and out of the organization and how they progress between the various levels or grades. It records stocks – the number of people employed in each occupation or grade in lengths of service or career bands; and flows – leavers, recruits and promotions – again by occupation and grade, and according to length of service.

This information describes the human resource system, and modelling techniques can be used to evaluate the outcomes of alternative assumptions about the future behaviour of the system.

The stocks and flows analysis, together with data on future requirements and the potential of existing employees, can be used for the production of management succession schedules and for planning career moves and development programmes.

External market analysis

The external market analysis should study the following.

- *The local labour market,* to obtain information on the supply of school leavers, the availability of key skills, population trends, training facilities, demand for skills by other employers and existing job vacancies.
- *The regional labour market,* to obtain the same information as for the local labour market over a wider area.
- *The national labour market,* to obtain information on demographic trends and their implications on the supply of school leavers, graduates and professionally qualified people. Trends in the national supply and demand for key skills should be analyzed to identify potential shortages. National training initiatives and trends in occupational structuring should also be studied.

RESOURCING PLANS

Resourcing plans will cover:

- *recruitment* – numbers and sources of recruits, specifications of skill, attitudinal and behavioural requirements, methods of attracting candidates;

- *retention* – increasing commitment to stay with the company;
- *downsizing* – if necessary, plans for reducing numbers as humanely as possible (through natural wastage);
- *training and retraining* – to supply skills or increase and widen skill levels.

The plans may have to deal specifically with skill shortages and reductions in the number of young people entering the labour market. The following measures can be considered:

- improving methods of identifying the sort of people the organization wants;
- establishing better links with schools and colleges to gain their interest;
- liaising closely with local training organizations – in the UK this will mean the local TEC (Training Enterprise Council);
- developing career programmes and training packages to attract young people;
- widening the recruitment net to include, for example, more women entering the labour market;
- finding ways of tapping alternative pools of suitable workers;
- adapting working hours and arrangements to the needs of new employees;
- providing more attractive benefit packages;
- providing child-care facilities;
- developing the talents and making better use of existing employees;
- providing retraining to develop different skills;
- making more effort to retain staff.

IMPROVING THE EFFECTIVENESS OF RECRUITMENT

Overall, an HRM approach to recruitment involves taking much more care in matching people to the requirements of the organization as a whole, as well as to the particular needs of the job. And these requirements will include commitment and ability to work effectively as a member of a team.

Examples of this approach in Japanese companies in the UK include the establishment of the Nissan plant in Washington, Tyne and Wear and Kumatsu in Newcastle upon Tyne. As described by Townley (1989), both followed a conscious recruitment policy with rigorous selection procedures. Aptitude tests, personality questionnaires and group exercises were used and the initial prescreening device was a detailed 'biodata' type questionnaire which enabled the qualifications and work history of candidates to be assessed and rated systematically. Subsequent testing of those who successfully completed the first stage was designed to assess individual attitudes, as well as aptitude and ability. As Wickens (1987) said of the steps taken at Nissan to achieve commitment and teamworking:

> It is something which develops because management genuinely believes in it and acts accordingly – and recruits or promotes people who have the same belief.

The need for a more sophisticated approach to recruitment along these lines is characteristic of HRM. The first requirement, as discussed below, is to take great care in specifying the competences, attitudes and behavioural characteristics required of employees. The second is to use a wider range of methods to identify candidates who match the specifications.

As a device for predicting success in a job, the traditional unstructured interview is inadequate. Other methods such as ability tests and biodata have greater validity. A study was made by Hunter and Hunter (1984) of the validity of alternative methods as predictors of performance for people moving into their first job. If total validity is achieved (ie 100 per cent accuracy in prediction) the score (the correlation coefficient) would be 1.00. The mean validity (a statistical method for comparing and averaging results over a large number of studies) actually achieved by these methods was:

ability tests	0.53
biodata	0.37
interview	0.14
academic achievements	0.11
education	0.10
age	−0.01

Personality questionnaires were shown to have the low validity coefficient of 0.15 on the basis of research conducted by Schmitt *et al* (1984). But, as Saville and Sik (1992) point out, this was based on a rag-bag of tests, many developed for clinical use and some using 'projective' techniques such as the Rorschach inkblots test, the interpretation of which relies on a clinician's judgement and is therefore quite out of place in a modern selection procedure. Smith's (1988) studies based on modern self-respect questionnaires revealed an average validity coefficient of 0.39.

The following rule-of-thumb guide was produced by Smith (1984) on whether a validity coefficient is big enough:

over 0.5	excellent
0.40–0.49	good
0.30–0.39	acceptable
less than 0.30	poor

On this basis, only ability tests, biodata and (according to Smith's figures) personality questionnaires reach acceptable levels of validity.

It is generally accepted that higher levels of validity can be attained if the selection process uses a wider range of methods than just an interview. These may be brought together in an assessment centre.

The rest of this section discusses methods of specifying requirements in the form of competences and the use of tests, biodata and assessment centres or group selection procedures.

Specifying competences

Competences can be defined in broad terms as the behavioural dimensions affecting job performance. They refer to the capacities people have, what they must be able to do and how they are expected to behave in order to meet the requirements of the job within the context of the organization – its culture (values and norms), business strategy and working environment.

When defining competences it is therefore necessary, in the first place, to determine the particular knowledge, skills and qualities required by individuals in order successfully to achieve their job objectives. But it is also necessary to analyze the organizational context with a view to assessing what behavioural characteristics would be appropriate. This includes the strategic characteristics of the organization, which should determine policies not only on the particular type of people the business requires, but also how they should be found and developed.

A competence analysis is often based on interviews and/or question-naires, although a 'workshop' approach can be adopted in which a number of people who are in the jobs under consideration or have extensive knowledge of them, get together as a group to carry out the analysis. In addition, or alternatively, the analysis can be based on a study of existing employees to establish any correlation between assessed performance levels and the knowledge, skills, abilities or behavioural characteristics they possess.

Job requirements

When conducting a competence analysis, it is first necessary to concentrate on what people do, the situations they face and, importantly, what distinguishes the behaviour of people at different levels of competence. The questions to be asked include the following.

- What is the job holder expected to accomplish in terms of objectives, targets and standards of performance?
- What are the positive or negative indicators of behaviour which are conducive or non-conducive to achieving objectives? In a managerial position, for example, the headings to be considered might include:

—   personal drive;
—   impact;
—   ability to communicate;
—   team management and leadership;
—   ability to work as a member of a team;
—   interpersonal skills;
—   analytical power;
—   ability to innovate (creative thinking);
—   strategic thinking;
—   commercial judgement;
—   ability to adapt and cope with change and pressure.

These indicators should be illustrated by specific instances of effective or less effective behaviour.

■   What are the specific areas of knowledge and skills required to achieve a competent level of performance in this job?
■   What sort of education, training and qualifications are likely to provide the levels of knowledge and skills required?
■   What type of experience and how much of it is required to achieve a competent level of performance?

Organizational requirements

It is also necessary to analyze organizational requirements, which means assessing the organization's strategies as they affect the sort of people it needs, its culture, its management style and its working climate. The sort of questions that should be asked include the following.

■   At what stage in its life cycle is this organization – is it growing, has it reached maturity or is it in need of regeneration?
■   What sort of organization is it – to what extent is it entrepreneurial, dynamic, innovative or bureaucratic, mechanistic, unadventurous?
■   What is the culture of the organization in terms of its values and norms – how much importance is attached to teamwork, quality, flexibility, caring for people's individual needs, providing a high quality of working life?
■   What is the prevailing management style – to what extent is it autocratic, democratic, task/result oriented, people oriented?
■   To what extent does the organization want people who will fit its culture? How far is it prepared to accept deviations from the norm?

Matching the business strategy

As Chandler (1962) remarked in his classic study of American industrial enterprise, 'structure follows strategy'. What the organization is and sets out to do not only determines its organization structure, but also the type of people it wants. Key executives need to be matched to the business strategy and General Electric classifies its general managers in accordance with the well-known Boston Consulting Group's portfolio matrix:

Business type	General manager requirement
■ wildcat	■ grower
■ star	■ defender
■ cash cow	■ caretaker
■ dog	■ undertaker

A study of the General Electric portfolio might indicate, for example, that there is a shortage of growers for the wildcats and too many undertakers in growth areas. Appropriate resourcing action can then be taken.

Texas Instruments believes that it is necessary to match management style to product life cycle. As a product moves through different phases of its life cycle, different levels of management skills become dominant. It could be disastrous, for instance, to put risk-taking entrepreneurs in charge of mature cash cow businesses. It could be equally disastrous to put cost-cutting efficiency-oriented managers in charge of growing businesses where they might stifle initiative and prevent the business gaining market share.

A definition of the competences required in a start-up situation may state that the major requirements are to create a vision of the business, establish core technical and marketing expertise and build the management team.

The characteristics required for candidates for such a position might be:

- a clear view of the finished business;
- hands-on orientation, ie a 'do-er';
- skill in devising entry strategies and launching products;
- in-depth knowledge of critical technical areas;
- a broad knowledge of key business functions;
- high-level energy and stamina;
- organizing ability;
- teambuilding capabilities;
- staffing skills;
- personal magnetism and charisma.

In contrast, the major job requirements in a turnaround situation may be for a rapid and accurate problem diagnosis and the ability to fix short-term problems without prejudicing the future. The characteristics required of a chief executive in these circumstances would be strong analytical and diagnostic skills, an orientation towards 'taking charge', a strong leader, high energy level, a risk taker who handles pressure well and the possessor of good crisis management skills.

Miles and Snow (1978 and 1984) identified three types of strategic behaviour and supporting organizational characteristics in so far as they affect resourcing strategies and the specification of competences. Their categories comprise the following.

1 *Defender* These organizations carve out a niche in narrow, relatively stable markets. They depend heavily on the development of very efficient technology and production. Defenders devote few resources to basic research and development, choosing instead to focus on improving efficiency in technological and transformation processes. Managers tend to have narrow, specialised skills and are promoted from within. These organizations engage in a 'make' approach – they carry out relatively little recruiting above entry level, with selection based on 'weeding out undesirable employees', while training and development involve extensive skills-building programmes.

2 *Prospector* These organizations focus on identifying and exploiting new market opportunities. Innovation and adaptability are fostered through divisions or product structures, decentralized authority and overlapping divisions of labour. To be able to move quickly into new businesses, managerial talent is often acquired from outside the organization. Prospectors therefore tend to 'buy in' talent, a policy requiring sophisticated recruiting at all levels, with selection involving pre-employment psychological testing. Training is limited and the emphasis is on identifying skill requirements and acquiring them in the external labour market.

3 *Analyzer* These organizations operate in two different types of market. Like defenders, some areas are in relatively unchanging product markets. Others, however, watch their competition closely for new ideas and then move quickly to develop efficient production methods for those which appear most promising. To achieve effective coordination between the stable and dynamic domains, analyzers are frequently organized into matrix structures which combine both functional and product groups. Managerial talent is drawn from internal promotion, external recruitment, mergers and acquisitions. Analyzer companies therefore match recruitment, selection and development strategies to the nature of the product (stable, innovative) and the stage of the product life cycle. They engage in make or buy HRM policies as appropriate in the different market domains.

Job competences

Within the strategic framework which influences the competences required at all levels, it is possible to develop lists of the generic competences relevant for particular jobs. These can be used as criteria in assessment or development centres or a standard selection procedure. For example, an international group in the finance sector describes its effective managers as:

- achievement orientated – they are strongly motivated by achievement, recognition and reward, and possess an internal drive which continually urges them forward to higher levels;
- having a positive outlook – they are energetic, enthusiastic and want to make a unique personal contribution to every job they do;
- being reliable – they are noted for always doing a job properly with attention to relevant detail;
- being adaptable – they are flexible, self-organized and self-monitoring;
- being able to organize themselves and those around them to meet targets effectively and on time;
- having a natural affinity with people, well-developed leadership skills, and a high degree of maturity in dealing with others;
- understanding that their progress can be enhanced by building up the performance of their teams – they are therefore keen to advance the interests of others, as well as themselves;
- good communicators, both face to face and on paper.

At the individual job level, competence analysis identifies the following.

- *Inputs* – what the job holder needs to know and be able to do. This identifies knowledge and skill requirements.
- *Process* – how the job holder applies knowledge and skill to do the work. This identifies the behavioural requirements.
- *Outcomes* – the value added to the organization as a result of the job holder's contribution. This provides information on the job's value to the company.

Structured interviewing

The inadequacy of the interview as a predictor of performance arises because the standard of interviewing is generally low. This is not simply a result of many people using poor interviewing techniques (eg they talk rather than listen), but more importantly it is a result of not carrying out a proper analysis of the competences required, with the result that they do not know the information they need to obtain from the candidate as a basis for structuring the interview.

The framework of a structured interview is provided by a competences analysis which will produce data on what is needed in terms of knowledge, skills and behaviours. Questions are then framed to elicit information on the extent to which the candidate meets the specified requirements. The answers provided by interviewees are then assessed by means of specially developed rating scales. A behavioural approach will include focused questions on how the candidate would behave in situations which have been identified as critical to effective job performance. A typical interview may include about ten pre-prepared 'situational' questions. It was noted by Latham *et al* (1980) that interviews using this technique produced reasonably reliable and consistent assessments.

Tests

The purpose of a selection test is to provide an objective means of measuring individual abilities or characteristics. These involve the application of standard procedures to subjects which enable their responses to be quantified. The differences in the numerical scores represent differences in abilities or behaviour.

A good test has the following four characteristics.

1   It is a *sensitive measuring instrument* which discriminates well between subjects.

2   It has been *standardized* on a representative and sizeable sample of the population for which it is intended so that any individual's score can be interpreted in relation to that of others.

3   It is *reliable* in the sense that it always measures the same thing. A test aimed at measuring a particular characteristic, such as intelligence, should measure the same characteristic when applied to different people at the same or a different time, or to the same person at different times.

4   It is *valid* in the sense that it measures the characteristic which the test is intended to measure. Thus, an intelligence test should measure intelligence (however defined) and not simply verbal facility. A test meant to predict success in a job, or in passing examinations, should produce reasonably convincing (statistically significant) predictions.

If properly standardized and validated, selection tests (sometimes referred to as psychometric tests) can play an important part in an HRM-oriented recruitment procedure.

Norms can be established which are consistent with the competences and behavioural characteristics required to attain strategic goals, and either maintain the culture or achieve cultural change. People can be selected who are more likely to uphold key values such as teamwork and quality.

However, the validity level of tests, even if they have been carefully introduced, is limited. Even ability tests only achieve a validity coefficient of 0.53. But they can be combined with other methods to produce a more accurate prediction.

The main types of tests are as follows.

■   *Aptitude tests*, which are designed to predict the potential an individual has to perform a job or specific tasks within a job.

■ *Attainment tests*, which measure abilities or skills that have already
   been acquired by training or experience.
■ *Intelligence tests*, which measure such factors as verbal and abstract
   reasoning, and give an indication of the level of intellectual ability.
■ *Personality questionnaires*, such as Saville and Holdsworth's OPQ
   (occupational personality questionnaire), are used for the occupational assessment of personality, motivations, interests, attitudes and
   values. They typically involve the self-report technique. The validity
   of personality tests has been attacked vigorously but Saville *et al*
   (1991) concluded from the largest validation study involving managers ever reported in Britain that certain personality factors could be
   used as criteria of job success. But they warned that only specific and
   properly validated tests can produce useful predictions of likely
   success in particular jobs.

Biodata

Biodata has been defined by Owens (1976) as:

> scored autobiographical data which are objective or scorable items of
> information provided by an individual on previous experience
> (demographic, experiential, attitudinal) which can be presumed or
> demonstrated to be related to personality structure, personal adjust-
> ment, or success in social, educational or occupational pursuits.

The key points in this definition are that biodata are items of biographical
data which are criterion based and objectively scored and, by measurements of past behaviour, predict future behaviour.

The items of biodata consist of demographic details (sex, age, family
circumstances), education and professional qualifications, previous
employment history and work experience, positions of responsibility
outside work, leisure interests and career/job motivation. These items are
weighted according to their relative importance as predictors, and a range
of scores is allocated to each one. The biodata questionnaire (essentially a
detailed application form) obtains information on each item, which is then
scored.

Biodata are most useful when a large number of applicants are received
for a limited number of posts. Cut-off scores can then be determined, based
on previous experience. These scores would indicate who should be
accepted for the next stage of the selection process and who should be
rejected, but they would allow for some possible candidates to be held
until the final cut-off score can be fixed, after the first batch of applicants
have been screened.

Biodata criteria and predictors are selected by job analysis, which
produces a list of competences. The validity of these items as predictors
and the weighting to be given to them are established by analyzing the

biodata of existing employees who are grouped into high or low performers. As described by Strebler (1991), the weighting could be decided by establishing the percentage in each group whose biodata relate to a level of achievement or type of achievement for a particular item.

Weights are allocated to items according to the discriminating power of the response. For example, in Table 12.1, the percentages of item responses on degree subjects for high and low performers are computed and subtracted. Weights can be ascribed which are a function of the significant difference between the two criterion groups.

Table 12.1 *Weighting of a biodata item*

Item – degree subject	High group %	Low group %	Difference high–low	Weight
Engineering	55	35	20	2
Sciences	35	20	15	1
Arts	10	45	–35	0
	100	100		

Biodata questionnaires and scoring keys are usually developed for specific jobs in an organization. Their validity compares reasonably well with other selection instruments, but they need to be developed and validated with great care and they are only applicable when large groups of applicants have to be screened.

Assessment centres

Assessment centres use a range of assessment techniques to determine whether or not candidates are suitable for a particular job or for promotion. They can also be used to identify development needs. The aims and methods of assessment centres vary considerably according to the needs of the organization. There are, however, a number of typical features, which are as follows.

- The focus of the centre is on behaviour.
- Exercises are used to capture and simulate the key dimensions of the job. These include one-to-one role – plays and group exercises. It is assumed that performance in these simulations predicts behaviour on the job.
- Interviews and tests will be used in addition to group exercises.
- Performance is measured in several dimensions in terms of the competences required to achieve the target level of performance in a particular job or at a particular level in the organization.

- Several candidates or participants are assessed together to allow interaction, and to make the experience more open and participative.
- Several assessors or observers are used in order to increase the objectivity of assessments. Involving senior managers is desirable to ensure that they 'own' the process. Assessors must be carefully trained.

Assessment centres in an HRM environment provide good opportunities for indicating the extent to which candidates match the culture of the organization. This will be established by observations of their behaviour in different but typical situations, and the range of the tests and structured interviews which are part of the proceedings. Assessment centres also give candidates a better feel for the organization and its values so that they can decide for themselves whether or not they are likely to fit.

A well-conducted assessment centre can achieve a better forecast of future performance and progress than judgements made by line or even personnel managers in the normal, unskilled way.

ALTERNATIVE SOURCES

However important it is to use the most appropriate recruitment and selection methods, resourcing plans should also consider alternative ways of satisfying needs.

- *Training* – more emphasis on internal training programmes to provide the skills required.
- *Career management* – installing management development and career planning programmes to provide for management succession from within the company.
- *Productivity planning* – planning for improved productivity and therefore reduced employment costs. This can be done by improving or streamlining methods, procedures and systems, investing in new technology, introducing better financial incentives, and developing more effective managers and team leaders. In addition, greater commitment from employees to performance improvements can be gained by involvement programmes (eg quality circles) and special working arrangements such as autonomous work groups or high-performance work design.
- *Downsizing* – stripping out unnecessary layers of management, ensuring that the introduction of new technology, especially information technology, really does save jobs and recognizing that the extension of teamworking may reduce the need for the number of supervisors currently employed. It would, of course, be essential to ensure that a downsizing strategy, as described later in this chapter, incorporates plans to mitigate the effect on individuals, and that unavoidable redundancies are dealt with humanely.

- *Flexibility* – increasing flexibility by means of flexible working hours, the use of subcontracting, temporary workers and part-timers and the development of 'functional flexibility', ie giving employees appropriate training or retraining so they can be redeployed quickly to different activities.

RETENTION STRATEGY

Resourcing plans should attempt to reduce the number of people to be recruited (which can be expensive and time consuming), not only by taking steps to pursue alternative ways of satisfying needs, but also by taking steps to retain the people the organization wants to keep.

The retention strategy should be based on an analysis of why people leave. Exit interviews may provide some information but they are unreliable – people do not always give the full reasons for leaving. A better method is to conduct attitude surveys at regular intervals. A retention plan should address each of the following areas in which lack of commitment and dissatisfaction can arise.

- *Pay* – problems arise because of uncompetitive, inequitable or unfair pay systems.
- *Jobs* – dissatisfaction can arise if jobs are unrewarding in themselves, because they do not provide for skill variety, task significance, autonomy or feedback.
- *Performance* – employees can be demotivated because they are unclear about their responsibilities or performance standards, are not provided with feedback on how well they are doing, or feel that their performance appraisals are unfair.
- *Training* – turnover can increase if people are not trained properly, or feel that demands are being made on them that they cannot reasonably be expected to fulfil without proper training. New employees can go through an 'induction crisis' if they are not given adequate training when they join the organization.
- *Career prospects* – dissatisfaction with career prospects is a major cause of resignations. This may be unavoidable – more people now recognize that they need to broaden their experience in a number of organizations. But such wastage can be unnecessary if it is caused by a failure of the organization to keep individuals informed of their career prospects or to provide them with career development opportunities.
- *Commitment* – clearly, lack of commitment to the organization and its values can be a major underlying cause of poor retention rates.
- *Management and supervision* – a common reason for resignations is the feeling that management in general, or individual managers and supervisors in particular, are treating people unfairly or are not up to their jobs in the sense that they are not providing adequate leadership

or are failing to provide their staff with the support, guidance and encouragement they have the right to expect, or are treating people unfairly.

- *Recruitment and promotion* – rapid turnover can result from poor selection or promotion decisions which result in the capacities of people not being matched to the demands of the work they do.
- *Over-marketing* – jobs can be oversold. If the type of work people do, or the career and training opportunities do not match the promises made on recruitment, people will want to leave.

The remedy for these problems is to improve the organization's systems for recruitment, training and development, performance management and reward. In other words, it is necessary to develop a coherent and integrated approach to the employment of people, and this is the essence of human resource management. Much of the blame for poor retention rates, however, rests with managers and supervisors. They need to be briefed on their responsibilities for reducing unnecessary losses and given comprehensive training on how to exercise them. One of the key criteria for measuring their performance should be their success in achieving agreed standards of performance in these areas.

Chapter 13

Human Resource Development

THE SIGNIFICANCE OF HUMAN RESOURCE DEVELOPMENT

The essence of HRM is that employees are valued assets and that their value should be increased by a systematic and coherent approach to investing in their training and development. Resourcing is about providing the skills base needed by the organization. Human resource development (HRD) is about enhancing and widening these skills by training, by helping people to grow within the organization, and by enabling them to make better use of their skills and abilities. Resourcing and HRD policies are closely linked. Companies can operate a make or buy policy (or a combination of the two), growing their own skills or acquiring them from elsewhere.

As Keep (1989) says:

> One of the primary objectives of HRM is the creation of conditions whereby the latent potential of employees will be realized and their commitment to the causes of the organization secured. This latent potential is taken to include, not merely the capacity to acquire and utilize new skills and knowledge, but also a hitherto untapped wealth of ideas about how the organization's operations might be better ordered.

BENEFITS OF HUMAN RESOURCE DEVELOPMENT

Besides enlarging and developing the skills base of the organization, investment in HRD can provide the following benefits.

- *A signal* to employees that the company believes they are important.
- *Motivation* to acquire and use new skills for which they will be rewarded.
- *Commitment* by communicating to employees the values of the organization, for example quality and customer service, and ensuring that they learn how they should uphold them.

- *Identification* with the company by helping people to achieve a better understanding of its aims and policies.
- *Communication* – training can provide an effective channel for two-way communication, especially if 'workshops' are used to bring managers and employees together to discuss organizational issues and develop plans jointly to deal with them.
- *Need satisfaction* – training can contribute to the satisfaction of people's needs for achievement and recognition; to be singled out to attend a course can be a powerful motivator.
- *Job enrichment* through skills development – training can enable people to exercise greater responsibility, and can enlarge their portfolio of skills which they can use both to their own advantage and that of the company. For example, an important spin-off from the introduction of quality circles is the training given to their members in analytical, problem-solving and presentation skills.
- *Change management* – education and training are essential ingredients in a change management programme. They help people to understand why change is necessary and how they will benefit. They can equip them with the confidence to cope with change and the skills they need to implement it.

In short, human resource development empowers members of the organization to increase their contribution to its success while enabling them to build their skills and capacities simultaneously.

THE APPROACH TO HUMAN RESOURCE DEVELOPMENT

Human resource development involves:

- the use of systematic and planned training approaches;
- adopting a policy of continuous development;
- creating and maintaining a learning organization;
- ensuring that all training activities are performance related;
- paying particular attention to management development and career planning.

SYSTEMATIC AND PLANNED TRAINING

Systematic training

Systematic training is training which is specifically designed to meet defined needs. It is planned and provided by people who know how to train, and the impact of training is carefully evaluated.

Systematic training is based on a simple, four-stage model expressed as follows.

- define training needs;
- decide what sort of training is required to satisfy these needs;
- use experienced and trained trainers to plan and implement training;
- follow up and evaluate training to ensure that it is effective.

The model provides a good basis for planning training programmes, but it is oversimplified – training is a more complex process than this. Another drawback to the concept of systematic training is that insufficient emphasis is placed on the responsibilities of managers and individuals for training. The concept of planned training provides a more comprehensive description of the training process.

Planned training

Planned training as defined by Kenney and Reid (1988), is 'a deliberate intervention aimed at achieving the learning necessary for improved job performance'. The process of planned training consists of the following steps.

1   *Identify and define training needs* – this involves analyzing corporate, team, occupational and individual needs to acquire new skills or knowledge, or to improve existing competences (competence is defined as the ability and willingness to perform a task). The analysis covers problems to be solved, as well as future demands. Decisions are made at this stage on the extent to which training is the best and most cost-effective way to solve the problem.

2   *Define the learning required* – it is necessary to specify as clearly as possible what skills and knowledge have to be learnt, and what attitudes need to be developed.

3   *Define the objectives of training* – learning objectives are set which define not only what has to be learnt, but also what trainees must be able to do after their training programme.

4   *Plan training programmes* – these must be developed to meet the needs and objectives by using the right combination of training techniques and locations.

5   *Decide who provides the training* – the extent to which training is provided from within or outside the organization will be decided. At the same time, the decision of responsibility between the training department, managers or supervisors and individuals has to be determined.

6   *Implement the training* – ensure that the most appropriate methods are used.

CONTINUING DEVELOPMENT

Training has to be planned properly, but a philosophy of continuing development states that training is not just something which is provided for people by the organization at the start of their employment or at occasional points in their career. It should instead be regarded as a continuing process, with less emphasis on formal instruction and an increased requirement for trainees to be responsible for their own learning, with help and guidance from their managers.

The Institute of Personnel Management's 1987 code of practice on continuous development states:

> If learning activity in an organization is to be fully beneficial both to the organization and its employees, the following conditions must be met.
>
> - The organization must have some form of strategic business plan. It is desirable that the implications of the strategic plan, in terms of the skills and knowledge of the employees who will achieve it, should be spelled out.
> - Managers must be ready and willing (and able) to define and meet needs as they appear. All learning needs cannot be anticipated; organizations must foster a philosophy of continuous development.
> - As far as practicable, learning and work must be integrated. This means that encouragement must be given to all employees to learn from the problems, challenges and successes inherent in their day-to-day activities.
> - The impetus for continuous development must come from the chief executive and other members of the top management team (the board of directors, for example). The top management team must regularly and formally review the way the competences of its management and workforce are being developed. It is important, too, that one senior executive is charged with responsibility for ensuring that continuous development activity is being effectively undertaken.
> - Investment in continuous development must be regarded by the top management team as being as important as investment in research, new product development or capital equipment. It is not a luxury which can be afforded only in the good times. Indeed, the more severe the problems an organization faces, the greater the need for learning on the part of its employees and the more pressing the need for investment in learning.

CREATING A LEARNING ORGANIZATION

A learning organization has been defined by Pedlar *et al* (1989) as 'an organization which facilitates the learning of all its members and continually transforms itself'. Handy (1989) describes a learning organization as one that both learns and encourages learning in people. It creates space for people to question, think and learn, and constantly reframes the world and their part in it. The learning organization, according to Handy, needs to have a formal way of asking questions, seeking out theories and reflecting on them. Members of the organization must be encouraged to challenge traditional ways of doing things and suggest improvements.

All successful companies are good at doing certain things. This is their knowledge and skills base. This base must be developed to match changing conditions. Learning is not just the acquisition of new knowledge; it is, rather, a collective process of observation, experimentation and experience, which can be mobilized to deal with new opportunities or threats.

It is necessary for companies to 'make space' in meetings, workshops and conferences, so that people can reflect on what they have learned and need to learn. But what needs to be learned cannot always be taught. Human resource development programmes must therefore help people to learn from their experience. Learning cannot be left to chance.

The characteristics of a learning organization are that it:

■ encourages people to identify and satisfy their own learning needs;
■ provides individuals with regular reviews of performance and learning needs;
■ provides feedback on performance and achieved learning;
■ provides new experiences from which people can learn;
■ facilitates the use of training on the job.

PERFORMANCE-RELATED TRAINING

A performance-related approach to training relates training specifically to performance requirements. For individuals this may mean filling gaps between what they know and *can* do, and what they *should* know and be able to do. But concentrating on filling gaps may mean falling into the trap of adopting the 'deficiency model' of training, which implies that training is only about putting right the things that have gone wrong.

Training is much more positive than that. It is, or should be, more concerned with identifying and satisfying development needs – multi-skilling, fitting people to take on extra responsibility, providing for management succession and increasing all-round competence.

Performance-related training also relates to organizational needs. These will be concerned with ensuring that employees have the necessary knowledge and skills to be able to take on new tasks as the company grows, diversifies, develops new products, markets and operational systems, and introduces new technology.

Essentially, performance-related training is competence based. It starts from an analysis of the competences required for successful performance, now and in the future, assesses the areas in which competences need to be developed, and plans and installs training programmes or processes, such as performance management, to create the levels of competence required.

MANAGEMENT DEVELOPMENT

What is management development?

Management development aims to ensure that the organization has the effective managers it requires to meet its present and future needs. It is concerned with improving the performance of existing managers, giving them opportunities for growth and development, and ensuring, as far as possible, that management succession within the organization is provided for.

The objectives of management development are to increase the effectiveness of the organization by:

- improving the performance of managers by seeing they are clearly informed of their responsibilities, and by agreeing with them objectives against which their performance will be measured;
- identifying managers with further potential and ensuring they receive the required development, training and experience to equip them for more senior posts within their own locations and elsewhere in the organization;
- assisting chief executives and managers throughout the organization to provide adequate succession, and to create a system whereby this is kept under regular review.

Formal approaches to management development

The formal approaches to management development include the following.

- *Development on the job*, through coaching, counselling, monitoring and feedback by managers on a continuous basis associated with the use of performance management systems to identify and satisfy development needs.
- *Development through work experience*, which includes job rotation, job enlargement, taking part in project teams or task groups, 'action learning' and secondment outside the organization.
- *Formal training*, by means of internal or external courses which are used to teach new skills or help people to acquire additional knowledge, but aim to supplement experience rather than replace it.

■ *Structured self-development*, by following self-development pro-grammes agreed with the manager or a management development adviser – these may include guided reading or the deliberate extension of knowledge or acquisition of new skills on the job.

The formal approaches to management development are based on the identification of development needs through a performance management system or an assessment centre. The approach may be structured around a list of competences which have been defined as being appropriate for managers in the organization.

A typical list of managerial competences as compiled by Henley Management College is as follows.

Intellectual	Strategic perspective
	Analysis and judgement
	Planning and organizing
Interpersonal	Managing staff
	Persuasiveness
	Assertiveness and decisiveness
	Interpersonal sensitivity
	Oral communication
Adaptability	Adaptability and resilience
Results orientation	Energy and initiative
	Achievement motivation
	Business sense

Informal approaches to a management development

Informal approaches to management development make use of the learning experiences which managers meet during the course of their everyday work. Managers are learning every time they are confronted with an unusual problem, an unfamiliar task or a move to a different job. They then have to evolve new ways of dealing with the situation. They will learn if they analyze what they did to determine how and why it contributed to its success or failure. This retrospective or reflective learning will be effective if managers can apply it successfully in the future.

This is potentially the most powerful form of learning. The question is – can anything be done to help managers make the best use of their experience? This type of 'experiential' learning comes naturally to some managers. They seem to absorb, unconsciously, and by some process of osmosis, the lessons from their experience, although in fact they have probably developed a capacity for almost instantaneous analysis, which they store in their mental databank and which they can retrieve whenever necessary.

Ordinary mortals, however, either find it difficult to do this sort of analysis or do not recognize the need. This is where formal, or at least semi-formal, approaches can be used to encourage and help managers to learn more effectively. These approaches include:

- emphasizing self-assessment and the identification of development needs by getting managers to assess their own performance against agreed objectives and analyze the factors contributing to effective or less effective performance – this can be provided through a performance management system;
- getting managers to produce their own development plans;
- encouraging managers to discuss their own problems and opportunities with their bosses or colleagues in order to establish for themselves what they need to learn or be able to do.

CAREER MANAGEMENT

Definition

Career management plans and shapes the progression of individuals within an organization in accordance with assessments of organizational needs and the performance, potential and preferences of individual members of the enterprise.

Career management has three overall aims:

- to ensure that the organization's needs for management succession are satisfied;
- to provide men and women of promise with a sequence of training and experience that will equip them for whatever level of responsibility they have the ability to reach;
- to give individuals with potential the guidance and encouragement they need if they are to fulfil their potential and achieve a successful career with the organization in tune with their talents and aspirations.

Career management policies

Career management policies cover the following areas.

Make or buy decisions

The organization needs to decide on the extent to which it:

- makes or grows its own managers (a promotion from within policy);
- recruits or buys in deliberately from outside (bringing 'fresh blood' into the organization), which means adopting a policy that accepts a reasonable amount of wastage and even takes steps in good time to encourage people, fairly gently, to develop their careers elsewhere if they are in danger of stagnating;

- will have to buy in talent from outside because of future shortfalls in the availability of managers, as revealed by the demand and supply forecasts.

A make or buy policy may be expressed as follows: 'We plan to fill about 80 per cent of our management vacancies from within the organization. The remaining 20 per cent we expect to recruit from outside.'

Short or long-term policies

Policies for determining the time-scale for investing in careers fall into one or other of the following categories.

- *Short-term performance* – employers who adopt, consciously or unconsciously, this policy, concentrate on the 'here and now'. They recruit and train high performers who will be good at their present job and are rewarded accordingly. If they are really good, they will be promoted – there are plenty of opportunities – and the enterprise will get what it wants. Deliberately to train managers for a future that may never happen is considered a waste of time. Top managers in this type of organization may well say: 'If we can get good people to do work, the future will take care of itself. They'll prove and mature their abilities in their present job, and be ready and indeed eager to take on extra responsibilities when the occasion arises. The future can take care of itself. If there's no one around at the time, then we'll buy in someone from outside – no problem!'
- *Long-term plans* – employers who believe in long-term career planning develop highly structured approaches to career management. They go in for elaborate reviews of performance and potential, assessment centres to identify talent or confirm that it is there, 'high-flyer' schemes, and planned job moves in line with a predetermined programme.
- *Long-term flexibility* – employers who follow this policy appreciate that they must concentrate on getting good performance now, and that in doing so they will, to a considerable extent, be preparing people for advancement. To this extent, they adopt the same attitude as short-term employers. However, they also recognize that potential should be assessed and developed by training which is not job-specific, and by deliberately broadening experience through job rotation or the direction of career paths. This approach avoids the possible short-sightedness of the here-and-now policy and the rigidity and, often, lack of realism, inherent in the structured system. But in conditions of rapid development and change, how far is it actually possible to plan careers over the long term? The answer must be, to a very limited extent, except in a static organization which has implicitly recognized that it provides a 'cradle-to-grave' career for people who, in general, are willing to wait for 'Buggins's turn.

As a generalization, the short-term system is likely to be more common in smallish, rapidly growing, 'organic' businesses where form follows function and the organization is fluid and flexible. The longer-term system is more prevalent in larger, bureaucratic, 'mechanistic' types of organization, where accurate forecasts of future needs can be made, significant changes in skill requirements are not likely to take place and there is a steady flow, according to easily assessed performance, up the promotion ladder. Long-term flexibility is the approach used in strategic planning-oriented organizations which appreciate that the HRM approaches they have developed must be adaptive and flexible.

Chapter 14

Performance Management

PERFORMANCE MANAGEMENT – DEFINITION

Performance management can be defined as a process or set of processes for establishing shared understanding about what *is* to be achieved, and of managing and developing people in a way which increases the probability that it *will* be achieved in the short and longer term.

Overall aim

The overall aim of performance management is to establish a culture in which individuals and groups take responsibility for the continuous improvement of business processes, and of their own skills and contributions.

Performance management systems can be used to communicate and reinforce the organization's strategies, values and norms, and to integrate individual and corporate objectives. But they also enable individuals to express their own views on what they should be doing, where they should be going and how they should be managed. Thus, they provide a means whereby expectations can be shared between managers and their staff. Managers can clarify their expectations of what they want their staff to do and staff can communicate their expectations on how they should be treated. The aim is to achieve agreement because, as Fletcher (1984) put it: 'Our perceptions of what is real and valid in the world depend on a consensus of shared beliefs'.

In their extensive research into the operation of performance management systems, Bevan and Thompson (1991) noted the emergence of their use as an integrating process which meshes various human resource management activities with the business objectives of the organization. They identified two broad thrusts towards integration.

■ *Reward-driven integration*, which emphasizes the role of performance payment systems in changing organizational behaviour and tends to undervalue the part played by other human resource development (HRD) activities. This appears to be the dominant mode of integration being pursued in the United Kingdom.

■ *Development-driven integration*, which stresses the importance of ensuring that appropriate HRD activities are in place to meet the long-term objectives of the organization and, furthermore, to ensure business needs and HRD are coordinated. Although performance pay may operate in these organizations, it is perceived to be complementary to HRD activities, rather than dominating or driving them.

Bevan and Thompson suggest that the more limited reward-driven approach may reinforce 'a disposition to short-termism and set back organizational effectiveness in the long term'.

Specific aims

The specific aims of performance management are to:

■ achieve sustainable improvements in the organizational performance;
■ enable individuals to develop their abilities, increase their job satisfaction and achieve their full potential to their own benefit and that of the organization as a whole;
■ develop constructive and open relationships between individuals and their managers in a process of continuing dialogue, which is linked to the work actually being done throughout the year;
■ provide a framework for the agreement of objectives as expressed in targets and standards of performance, so that mutual understanding of these objectives and the role both managers and individuals have to play in achieving them, is increased;
■ provide for the accurate and objective measurement and assessment of performance in relation to agreed targets and standards, so that individuals receive feedback from managers on how well they are doing;
■ on the basis of this assessment, to enable individuals with their managers to: agree improvement plans and methods of implementing them, and jointly review training and development needs and agree how they should be satisfied;
■ provide an opportunity for individuals to express their aspirations and concerns about their work;
■ provide a basis for rewarding people in relation to their contribution by financial and/or non-financial means – the former consisting of performance related pay, and the latter including recognition of achievement and opportunities to take on more responsibility or enhance knowledge and skills.

PERFORMANCE MANAGEMENT AND HRM

Performance management systems can satisfy a number of the fundamental aims of HRM, namely, to:

- achieve sustained high levels of performance from its human resources;
- develop people to their full capacity and potential;
- establish an environment in which the latent potential of employees can be realized;
- reinforce or change the organization's culture.

Performance management is also concerned with the interrelated processes of work, management, development and reward. It can become a powerful integrating force, ensuring that these processes are linked together properly as a fundamental part of the human resource management approach, which should be practised by every manager in the organization.

THE PHILOSOPHY OF PERFORMANCE MANAGEMENT

The philosophy of performance management is based upon the following concepts:

- the need for a process of management which supports the achievement of the business strategy by integrating individual and corporate objectives;
- the need to develop and maintain, within the organization, a process which enables it to fulfil its responsibilities to employees;
- the need to enable employees to manage their own performance;
- the importance of creating a partnership between managers and their staff in managing performance – managing by agreement rather than by command;
- the use of objectives to provide the basis for measurement, assessment and development;
- the importance of measurement, feedback, positive reinforcement and 'contingency management' in managing performance;
- the significance of the input → process → output → outcome sequence in measuring and reviewing performance;
- the need to have a fair and equitable system for measuring and assessing performance, and for rewarding staff accordingly;
- the importance of recognizing that performance management is an essential process of *management*, and not just a glorified technique of performance appraisal and motivation.

Achieving the business strategy

An effective performance management system should develop employees' understanding of what needs to be achieved, help them to improve corporate performance and reward them on the basis of their contribution.

The role of performance management in supporting the achievement of the business strategy is fulfilled by providing a means of cascading corporate objectives downwards throughout the organization. The objectives set for senior managers are directly related to what they and the division, function, unit or department they control need to achieve to contribute fully to the attainment of corporate strategies. Senior managers in turn agree objectives with the members of their management team, spelling out the contribution the latter are expected to make in enabling their division, function etc to meet its targets.

This process is repeated at each level of the organization, so that the objectives agreed there are consistent with those agreed for the next higher layer. This provides for a link between the objectives set for office and shop floor workers, and other employees, who are responsible for basic organizational activities and those set at corporate level.

Clearly, the fewer levels there are the greater the chance of achieving consistency throughout the organization; and this is one of the most powerful arguments for 'flatter' organization structures.

Accompanying this process of 'delayering' organizations, there is a general trend towards pushing more accountability downwards. This is forcing line managers to introduce better ways of planning and budgeting, and in this environment they have to take objective setting more seriously.

Fulfilling organizational responsibilities

The organization has the corporate responsibility for enabling its employees to contribute to the satisfaction of both their own needs and those of the organization. Besides setting clear corporate objectives and individual or team targets, this requires the implementation of a policy of human resource development, as described in Chapter 13, which provides for coaching, counselling and training on a continuing basis.

Enabling employees to manage their own performance and development

Performance management is not just a system driven by management to manage the performance of their employees. Rather it is a process which enables employees to manage their own performance and development within the framework of clear objectives and standards which have been agreed with their managers. This does not absolve management from their responsibility to 'empower' employees through counselling and training. But it does place people in a situation where they are more in control of the consequences of their actions. This can increase their sense of responsibility. It also helps them to achieve what Maslow (1954) refers to as 'self-actualization', which he defined as 'the need to develop potentialities and skills; to become what one believes one is capable of becoming'.

Performance management can therefore help people to develop themselves and this accords with Drucker's (1955) view that:

Development is always self-development. Nothing could be more absurd than for the enterprise to assume responsibility for the development of a man. The responsibility rests with the individual, his abilities, his efforts.

But he goes on to say:

Every manager in a business has the opportunity to encourage individual self-development or to stifle it, to direct it or to misdirect it. He should be specifically assigned the responsibility for helping all men working with him to focus, direct and apply their self-development efforts productively.

Management by agreement

The essence of the performance management process is that it is a partnership between managers and the individuals who are members of their teams. This means that at every stage the aim is to obtain agreement on objectives, on the means of measuring performance, on the assessment of results and the factors affecting them, and on development and performance improvement plans.

This is management by agreement rather than management by command. It is in line with McGregor's (1960) principle of 'management by integration and self-control'. And it implies that there is shared accountability between managers and individuals for improving performance.

The importance of objectives

As Williams (1991) has written:

The setting of objectives is the management process which ensures that every individual employee knows what role they need to play and what results they need to achieve to maximise their contribution to the overall business. In essence it enables employees to know what is required of them and on what basis their performance and contribution will be assessed.

It is also suggested by Williams that objectives should:

- be jointly agreed in advance between the manager and the individual as both realistic and challenging and, as such, they are 'owned';
- measure the actual level of achievement so that the basis on which performance is assessed can be understood in advance and is as clear as possible;
- support the overall business strategies of the company so that the objectives, taken together, are mutually supportive and consistent throughout the organization.

At ICL, managers use three types of objectives.

1   Objectives which contribute to the achievement of the business objectives – *key result areas*.

2   Objectives which contribute to an improvement in the performance of the individual – *performance standards*.

3   Objectives which contribute to the development of the individual – *performance development*.

Objectives can be agreed following discussions between managers and the individuals or teams responsible to them. Teams may have joint objectives, and individuals who work together can agree common or overlapping objectives. Some organizations are now developing systems for internal customers to set objectives for internal suppliers of services.

Objectives provide the base for four key areas of performance management philosophy: measurement; feedback; positive reinforcement; and contingency management.

Measurement

Measurement requires the collection of performance data to establish a starting point or base line. To improve performance you must know what current performance is.

It is often said that anything which can be managed can be measured. But there is an element of truth in the adage that, in some jobs, what is meaningful is not measurable and what is measurable is not meaningful.

Measurement is obviously easier when financial, sales or production targets can be set. Subjectivity clearly increases when qualitative objectives are used. But it is still possible to agree firm standards of performance which define the conditions under which a job can be said to have been well done, and there have been many developments in recent years in, for example, measurement of service quality and customer satisfaction. The notion that employee performance should be measured, at least in part, on the basis of customer satisfaction returns, reports of 'mystery shoppers' in stores, or telephone customer surveys, is well established in several organizations. In the UK, BT, IBM and Whitbread are examples of prominent organizations taking this approach. Performance management is now supporting total quality management and customer service initiatives with firm performance measures.

Feedback

Measurement is followed by feedback, so that people can monitor their performance and, as necessary, take corrective action. As much feedback as possible should be self-generated. The philosophy of performance management emphasizes the importance of employees planning how they are going to achieve their objectives, and then obtaining feedback data themselves. The rapid development of management information systems in recent years has increased the capacity to provide quantitative and timely feedback. This applies in all areas. For example, cellular manufacturing systems using computer numerically controlled machines can generate instant feedback to the autonomous working groups in each unit of the system.

Reinforcement

Positive reinforcement is provided when behaviour which leads to improved performance is recognized. The object is to recognize specific performance improvements as soon as possible after the event. This is why performance management should be regarded as a continuing process. Recognition, and therefore reinforcement, takes place whenever appropriate throughout the year. It is not deferred to an annual performance appraisal session.

Similarly, if someone makes a mistake, or fails to deliver the agreed standard of performance, this should be discussed immediately so that learning can take place and improvement plans can be agreed. There should be no surprises in a performance appraisal meeting. If anything has gone wrong it should be pointed out at the time so that immediate corrective action can be taken.

As Handy (1989) suggests, reinforcement theory is about 'applauding success and forgiving failure'. He suggests that mistakes should be used as an opportunity for learning: 'something only possible if the mistake is *truly* forgiven because otherwise the lesson is heard as a reprimand and not as an offer of help.'

Contingency management

The concept of 'contingency management' refers to the belief that every behaviour has a consequence. When someone knows that desirable consequences are contingent upon good performance, they are more likely to improve. This is in line with the valency–instrumentality–expectancy theory formulated by Vroom (1964). Valency stands for value, instrumentality is the belief that if we do one thing it will lead to another, and expectancy is the probability that action will lead to an outcome.

The philosophy of performance management is largely based on this theory. The agreement or contract between managers and individuals spells out expectations of what is to be achieved, and the sort of behaviour required to achieve it. Implicitly or explicitly, there is an understanding either of the reward that will follow if the expected outcome is attained, or of the penalty that will be exacted if it is not. Rewards or penalties are contingent upon certain behaviours resulting in certain outcomes.

The input, process, output, outcome model

Performance management is concerned with:

- *inputs* – the skills, knowledge and personal characteristics the individual applies to the job;
- *process* – how the individual behaves in carrying out the task;
- *outputs* – what is produced by the individual when the task has been completed;
- *outcomes* – the impact of what has been achieved by the individual's performance on the results of the team, unit, function and, ultimately, the organization. Outcomes are therefore defined by the effect an individual's contribution has beyond his or her particular job.

The distinction between inputs, process, outputs and outcomes can be illustrated by reference to the job of a training manager, one of whose objectives is to plan and deliver a new training programme. Performance on this task would be measured by reviewing:

- *inputs* – the knowledge and skill deployed by the training manager in planning the course;
- *process* – the effectiveness with which training skills were used in conducting and evaluating the course;
- *outputs* – the quality of the courses themselves, in terms of their content, presentation and administration;
- *outcomes* – the impact made by the training on the performance of participants.

Performance appraisal systems traditionally concentrated on inputs and, to a certain degree, process. They asked managers to assess personality traits and behaviour under such headings as initiative, willingness and relationships with people. The problem was that the ratings were highly subjective – there were no standards for exercising judgements on these characteristics. Managers were asked to 'play at being God' and they were not good at it.

The reaction to this was sparked off by McGregor (1957), followed by Rowe (1964). McGregor believed that the emphasis should be shifted from appraisal to analysis, and from the past to the future. The main factor in measuring performance should be the analysis of the behaviour required to achieve agreed results, not the assessment of personality.

Rowe's research revealed that managers did not like appraising staff on their personality characteristics and either did not do it all, or if they tried, were more likely to fail than succeed. On personality assessments she commented, 'No appraiser has the moral right to press judgement on these matters except in so far as they are directly and demonstrably relevant in the subordinate's job'.

The views of McGregor and Rowe were related to those expressed earlier by Drucker (1955), who coined the phrase 'management by objectives and self-control'. He wrote:

> An effectivè management must direct the vision and efforts of all managers towards a common goal. It must ensure that the individual manager understands what results are demanded of him. It must ensure that the superior understands what to expect of each of his subordinate managers. It must motivate each manager to maximum efforts in the right direction. And while encouraging high standards of workmanship, it must make them the means to the end of business performance rather than the ends in themselves.

In Drucker's view, this approach would ensure that individual and corporate objectives would be integrated.

The ideas of these writers and others, such as Humble (1970), led to the concept of management by objectives (M by O). The philosophical basis of this approach is immaculate, but it tended to become a mechanistic system which bogged managers down in paperwork. It was therefore largely discredited. It was replaced by the concept of 'results-oriented appraisal', which avoided the elaborate procedures associated with M by O. However, the effectiveness of both these systems suffered because they concentrated on outputs. They tended to expect managers to quantify the unquantifiable, so that targets became artificial and short term. They neglected the longer-term outcomes (which were often difficult to quantify) and, worse, they deflected the attention of assessors from the inputs and processes which produced the result. Thus, insufficient attention was paid to what is sometimes referred to as 'behaviour modification', that is, analyzing the behavioural factors contributing to outcomes and deciding what needs to be done to get better results by changing behaviour.

Performance management systems emphasize the importance of outcomes which the individual influences, as well as immediate outputs. They analyze inputs and processes to determine development and training needs, and provide the basis for performance improvement plans. They will be concerned with diagnosing correctly whether differential performance is a function of the individual's motivation or is a result of his or her ability. The way in which people are managed, the resources they are given and the external factors beyond their control are also taken into account.

The analysis and diagnosis will be closely linked to specifications of behavioural requirements. These will be focused on objectives related to the individual's job, but they will also deal with wider organizational objectives, especially those concerned with the support of values such as quality, customer service, teamworking and flexibility.

The philosophy of performance management is therefore holistic. It takes an all-embracing view of the constituents of good performance; how this contributes to desired outcomes at the departmental and organizational level, and what needs to be done to improve these outcomes. This is entirely consistent with the HRM philosophy of treating employees as valued assets, and investing in their management and development in order to enhance their value.

Performance management as a process of management

The philosophy of performance management is strongly influenced by the belief that it is a natural process of management. Its emphasis on analysis, measurement, monitoring performance and planning for performance improvements means that it is concerned with basic aspects of good practice with regard to the management of people. It is a system which should be driven by management so that it becomes part of their everyday working life and not an annual chore imposed upon them by the personnel department.

Performance management systems can help managers, in Handy's (1989) words, to:

- be teachers, counsellors and friends, as much or more than they are commanders, counsellors and judges;
- trust people to use their own methods to achieve the manager's own ends;
- delegate on the basis of a positive will to trust and to enable and a willingness to be trusted and enabled;
- become 'post-heroic' leaders who know that every problem can be solved in such a way as to develop other people's capacity to handle it.

However, the skills required by managers to operate a performance management system are often underestimated. They need to know how to set clear, measurable and achievable objectives. They have to be able to handle performance review meetings, in which they not only commend staff on their achievements (which is not too difficult), but also help them to recognize where their performance has been substandard and needs to be improved (which can be much harder).

Performance management implies a marked shift in the relationship between managers and their staff. The manager is faced with a new and more challenging situation: counselling skills; effective listening; good communication; and the ability to handle and encourage upward appraisal all come to the fore. In essence, the development of a performance management system leads directly on to the need for a more systematic approach to skills-based management development.

FEATURES OF PERFORMANCE MANAGEMENT SYSTEMS

As described by Bevan and Thompson (1991), a 'textbook' performance management system (PMS) exhibits the following features.

- the organization has a shared vision of its objectives, or a mission statement, which it communicates to all its employees;
- the organization sets individual performance management targets, which are related both to operating unit and wider organizational objectives;
- it conducts a regular, formal review of progress towards these targets;
- it uses the review process to identify training, development and reward outcomes;
- it evaluates the effectiveness of the whole process and its contribution to overall performance to allow changes and improvements to be made.

The textbook definition, however, overemphasizes the 'top-down' approach and oversimplifies the process of integrating individual and organizational goals (a highly desirable feature, but difficult to attain). It should also be recognized that each organization will need to develop its own approach to performance management in accordance with its culture and management processes. For example, some companies link performance management reviews directly with performance related pay as described in Chapter 15. Some split the review into two parts, one concentrating on development needs and the other measuring and rating performance to determine merit payments. Others, especially in the public and voluntary sectors, reject the idea of performance related pay altogether, and use the system purely for managerial and developmental purposes.

Some performance management systems place more emphasis than others on the opportunity they give for individuals to raise with their managers general questions concerning their work and aspirations. This can become a form of upward assessment in which individuals are encouraged to comment on any problems created by the ways in which they are managed and the resources made available to them; for example, the guidance and support they receive, the extent to which the authority they are given matches their accountability, or the facilities and equipment with which they are provided.

There are, however, certain characteristics which are shared by all systems which can truly be called performance management. These consist of the following.

- An *agreement* between managers and individuals on expected targets and/or standards of performance and other objectives. The agreement will aim to establish and/or increase mutual understanding and to make clear the roles of managers and individuals in achieving targets and/or standards or other objectives.

- A *method of assessment* of performance in relation to agreed targets and/or standards of performance and other objectives which is realistic and impartial. The assessment will aim to encourage individuals and their managers to exchange information, and comment on their achievements.
- A *plan of action*, which will enable individuals to make a new agreement with their managers. This might include:
  - a *confirmation* that targets and/or standards are being consistently achieved and remain appropriate;
  - the *identification* of improvement and/or development plans and methods for implementing them;
  - a *joint review* of training or development needs and opportunities, and methods for satisfying them;
  - an *opportunity* for individuals and their managers to take a more general approach to the individual's position and role within the organization. This may include the expression of aspirations, concerns and suggestions. It can, by mutual agreement, be informal and not recorded.
- The *operation* of the system as a continuous cycle, starting with the performance agreement, covering objectives and improvement and development plans, which leads to the continuing review stage in which performance is reviewed informally as necessary and changes made to the performance agreement. This is followed by the preparation for review stage during which the manager and individual separately prepare an agenda for the review meeting. Finally, the performance review meeting takes place at the end of the performance cycle when past performance is assessed and a new performance agreement is reached.

INTRODUCING PERFORMANCE MANAGEMENT

Performance management systems can promise more than they achieve. They can fail for four main reasons:

1. top management is not fully behind the scheme;
2. line management feels it is a waste of time and/or mishandle the objective-setting and review processes;
3. staff feel the scheme is having a detrimental rather than a beneficial effect; and
4. quality control is not exercised over the operation of the scheme.

These issues must be addressed through careful planning and pilot testing, thorough briefing, comprehensive training and the systematic monitoring of the scheme in operation.

Developing the scheme

The development programme should be driven by top management, although the HR director can play an important part in gaining their commitment. Managers and staff should be jointly involved in developing the scheme, again with the support and advice of the HR function. This should be done through a working party which has the responsibility for designing the scheme, and planning and executing its implementation.

Briefing

All concerned must be briefed thoroughly on the purpose of the scheme, how it operates, the part they will play and how they will benefit. The following is an example of briefing notes prepared for the managers of a large charity where the emphasis is on the developmental aspects of the scheme, as its name implies.

**Performance and Development Management System
Manager's Briefing Notes**

Introduction

I am going to discuss with you our new Performance and Development Management System. I shall cover:

- why we are introducing it;
- how it will operate;
- the part you will play;
- the benefits to you.

I shall be glad to answer any questions at any time during this meeting.

Why we are introducing the system

There are two main reasons for introducing the system.

1   We want to focus everyone's attention on what they are expected to achieve in their jobs and how best to achieve it.

2   We would like to help everyone to identify and satisfy their development needs – to improve performance and further their careers.

Principles of the system

The fundamental principles of the system are that it will:

- concentrate on developing strengths, as well as considering any performance problems;

- be based on open and constructive discussion;
- be an everyday and natural management process – not an annual form-filling exercise;
- be a positive process – looking to the future rather than dwelling on the past.

How the system will work

The system will work as follows.

- You and your manager will discuss and agree your objectives, action plans, and development and training needs – this is called the performance and development agreement.
- During the review period (normally 12 months) you and your manager will keep under review your progress in meeting your objectives – as necessary you will agree revisions to those objectives and your priorities.
- Towards the end of the review period you and your manager will prepare for the performance and development review meeting separately – deciding in advance on any points you wish to raise and noting these down on a preparation form.
- A review meeting will then be held at which you can discuss with your manager how you got on during the review period, and any other points you want to raise. You will then draw up a new performance agreement together.

The results of the review meeting will be recorded on the Performance Review Form – you will be able to see and comment on what has been written – this will be a summary of what has been agreed.

Your manager's manager will see the form and will add any comments he or she feels may be appropriate. You will also see these comments.

You and your manager will then retain your own copies of the review form – no other copies will be held by anyone else.

The part you will play

We hope that you will contribute to the success of this scheme in the following ways:

- by preparing carefully for the review – noting any points you want to raise with your manager;
- by entering into the spirit of the review meeting, which is intended to provide for a full, frank but friendly exchange of views about your job and your prospects;
- by thinking carefully about how you are going to achieve the objectives and plans agreed at the meeting;
- by reviewing how you are getting on during the year and agreeing any actions required.

The part managers will play

All managers will be expected to play their part with you in preparing for the meeting, reviewing your performance and drawing up your performance agreement. They are being specially trained in how to do this.

Benefits to you

We hope the system will benefit you by ensuring that:

■   you know what is expected of you;
■   you know how you stand;
■   you know what you need to do to reach your objectives;
■   you can discuss with your manager your present job, your development and training needs, and your future.

We also hope that it will give you the opportunity to raise with your manager any points you want to discuss about your job and your career prospects.

Training

It is essential to train everyone concerned in the operation of the scheme, ie both managers *and* their staff. Training should be given to them on how to set objectives, how to select and use performance measures, and how review meetings should be prepared for and conducted. Managers should be trained in counselling and coaching techniques.

Quality control

Quality control can be achieved by careful initial training, by managers' managers reviewing how performance agreements and reports are completed, and by the HR function monitoring the implementation of the scheme. Following the first complete cycle it is a good idea to conduct a survey of what both managers and their staff feel about how the scheme has worked.

THE ROLE OF THE HR FUNCTION

The HR function can stimulate the introduction of a performance management system and facilitate its development. It provides the training required and monitors its implementation. Fundamentally, however, a performance management system should be owned and driven by line managers and their staff.

Chapter 15

The HRM Approach to Reward Management

WHAT IS REWARD MANAGEMENT?

Reward management is the process of developing and implementing strategies, policies and systems which help the organization to achieve its objectives by obtaining and keeping the people it needs and by increasing their motivation and commitment.

Armstrong and Murlis (1991)

Reward management is not just about money. It is concerned with intrinsic, as well as extrinsic motivation; with non-financial, as well as financial rewards.

The reward management system should be designed to support the achievement of the organization's strategies. It should be based on a philosophy of reward which matches the culture of the organization, but can help to change that culture.

The non-financial reward system will satisfy individual needs for variety, challenge, responsibility, influence in decision making, achievement, recognition, skills development and career opportunities. All of these can be catered for by adopting an HRM approach, as described in this book.

The financial reward system will incorporate procedures for tracking market rates, valuing jobs, designing and maintaining pay structures, paying for performance and skill, and providing employee benefits. These are described in detail by Armstrong and Murlis (1991). This chapter concentrates on the ways in which both non-financial and financial systems can be developed within an HRM context.

FUNDAMENTAL CHARACTERISTICS OF THE HRM APPROACH TO REWARD MANAGEMENT

In an HRM setting, an organization's reward management system:

- supports the achievement of its strategies;
- is fully integrated with other human resource strategies;
- is based on a well-articulated philosophy – a set of aims and assumptions which are consistent with the organization's HRM philosophies, define the objectives it wants the reward system to achieve and underpins the ways in which it proposes to reward its employees;
- recognizes that if, to put it crudely, human resource management is largely about investments in human assets, from which a reasonable return is required, then it is proper to reward people differentially according to the rate of return they generate, ie their contribution (pay for performance);
- focuses on the development of employee skills and qualities and contributes actively to strengthening the human resource capabilities of the organization (pay for competence and for skill);
- is itself an integrated process which can operate flexibly;
- supports a number of HRM requirements.

The rest of this chapter discusses each of the characteristics in turn.

SUPPORTING THE ACHIEVEMENT OF STRATEGY

Reward systems contain powerful symbols which communicate, beyond their instrumental value, management's philosophy, attitudes and intent. They are designed to encourage behaviour which will contribute directly to the achievement of the organization's objectives. It has been suggested by Tichy *et al* (1982) that 'the reward system is one of the most under-utilized and mishandled managerial tools for driving organizational performance'.

Reward strategies should:

- be in line with corporate values and beliefs;
- emanate from business strategies and goals;
- be linked to business performance;
- drive and support desired behaviour;
- fit required management style.

They will be concerned mainly with the mix and level of rewards which the company should provide and the extent to which rewards should be differentiated according to performance, competence and skill.

INTEGRATING REWARD AND HRM STRATEGIES

Reward strategies can be important levers for change, but they will work best if they are a part of a mutually reinforcing system of human resource management initiatives in the resourcing, development and performance management fields. The reward management system should be planned and administered in ways which will complement other HRM systems.

Thus, resourcing strategies will identify the skills required by the organization; reward strategies will be concerned with the reward system which is most likely to attract and retain those skills. Human resource development strategies will consider broadly how the level of competence can be increased; reward strategies will address the question of how people will be motivated to extend their skills and how they will be rewarded when they have acquired them. Performance management strategies will deal with ways of measuring differential performance; reward strategies will determine how pay increases or other benefits should be related to performance assessments.

REWARD PHILOSOPHY

Managements base their reward policies on certain assumptions about pay, but they tend to avoid subjecting these assumptions to critical examination, and they neglect to evaluate the extent to which their reward systems fit them. This approach was highlighted by the IPM/NEDO research into incentive schemes in 1991 (Cannell and Woods, 1992), which indicated that companies often introduced incentive schemes without a clear statement on what they were expected to achieve, and then failed to evaluate their effectiveness (which, without a stated objective, would in any case, be difficult).

Reward philosophies should be based on the HRM proposition that the ultimate source of value is people. This means that, although the reward philosophy and systems have to fit the business needs, they should also respond creatively to the needs of the people in the business.

Fitting the reward philosophy to business needs

Fitting the reward philosophy to business needs means considering the following issues:

- what the organization and its members are good at doing and what they need to do to improve – and how rewards can make the good better and help to achieve improvement;
- what the organization and its members need to be able to do in the future – and how the reward system can help to achieve change;
- whose performance matters most – a small cadre of key performers or people at all levels in the organization;
- the balance between rewarding individual performance and trying to develop more effective teamworking – on the one hand it is necessary to avoid defining individual performance in a way which is so internally competitive that it disrupts teamwork, on the other hand,

the situation should be avoided in which poor individual performance can be hidden within the team;

- business unit versus corporate performance – pay systems reflecting only the more distant performance of the organization have little leverage over the performance of the individual, but if the focus is exclusively local it could undermine the development of the business as a whole;

- short term versus long term – payment systems which do not reflect immediate past performance lose effectiveness and credibility, and objectives that are focused on the period immediately ahead will have most bite, but the system must recognize that the business needs to develop employees and their skills over the longer term.

Fitting the reward system to individual needs

A primary aim of a reward management system is that of increasing the motivation of employees. This raises fundamental questions about what factors affect motivation, the role of money as a motivator and what influences employee satisfaction with the reward system.

Factors affecting motivation

Motivation is concerned with the strength and direction of behaviour. A well-motivated person is someone with clearly-defined goals who takes action which he or she expects will achieve these goals.

Motivation is inferred from or defined by goal-directed behaviour. It is anchored in two basic concepts: a) the *needs* operating within the individual; and b) the *goals* in the environment towards or away from which the individual moves. In its simplest form, the process of motivation is initiated by the conscious or unconscious recognition of an unsatisfied need. A goal is then established which, it is thought, will satisfy that need, and a course of action is determined that will lead towards the attainment of the goal. But, as goals are satisfied, new needs emerge and the cycle continues.

The degree to which people are motivated will depend not only upon the perceived value of the outcome of their actions – the goal or reward – but also upon their perceptions of the likelihood of achieving the reward; that is, their expectations. The more they can control the means to achieve their goals, the more likely they are to be highly motivated.

Higher effort and motivation therefore exist when employees perceive a strong link between effort, performance and rewards. The degree to which better performance is achieved depends partly on the strength of the need and the attractiveness of the goal. It also depends, to a large extent, on the expectations of employees that they will reach the goal. Additionally, they must have the necessary competence and understanding of the requirements of their job or role.

In short, for individuals to exert effort in anticipation of rewards, they must expect worthwhile rewards to follow the effort. This, in essence, is expectancy theory, which must be taken into account when designing performance-related pay schemes.

The basic requirements for job satisfaction may include comparatively higher pay, an equitable payment system, real opportunities for promotion, considerate, fair and participative managers, a reasonable degree of social interaction at work, pleasant working conditions and a high degree of control over work pace and work methods.

The degree of satisfaction obtained by individuals, however, depends largely upon their own needs and expectations, and the environment in which they work. But there is no proof that high satisfaction produces better performance. Indeed, it can be argued that it is better performance which produces more satisfaction.

So what produces better performance? Obviously, high motivation is a key factor but, when developing reward philosophies, it is as well to remember that motivation is a complex process – needs, goals and expectations vary widely between individuals, and everyone has his or her own idea on the best way to achieve goals and to satisfy expectations.

Motivation, however, is not the only factor. Ability is also important. In fact, performance can be regarded as a function of motivation multiplied by ability. The relationship is multiplicative; high motivation is useless without ability, and vice versa. This is one very good reason for establishing close links between reward, resourcing and human resource development policies.

Finally, in considering individual needs, the importance of the distinction between intrinsic and extrinsic motivation should be recognized.

- *Intrinsic motivation* relates to the self-generated factors which influence people to behave in a particular way; these include responsibility, (feeling that work is important and having control over one's own resources), freedom (space) to act, scope to use skills and abilities, interesting and challenging work, and opportunities for advancement.
- *Extrinsic motivation* relates to what is done to and for people to motivate them; it includes rewards such as more pay, praise or promotion, and punishments such as withholding pay, criticism or disciplinary action.

Extrinsic motivation can have an immediate effect, but it will not necessarily last for long. Intrinsic motivation is likely to have a deeper and longer-term effect, because it is inherent in individuals and not imposed from outside.

The role of money as a motivator

When determining reward philosophies the following questions need to be answered.

- How should money be used? For example, to provide direct incentives for performance and/or to recognize performance stimulated by other means?
- What other tools besides money does the organization have at its disposal which might be more effective and less costly to improve performance?

It is necessary, when considering the role of money, to distinguish between incentives and rewards. Incentives stimulate better performance in the future; rewards recognize good performance in the past. This process of recognition, however, is also an incentive.

Money undoubtedly motivates – it provides the carrot which most, if not all, people want. It is a powerful force, because it leads directly or indirectly to the satisfaction of many needs. It can act as an incentive to improve performance and as a reward which recognizes success in a highly tangible way.

Doubts were cast by Herzberg *et al* (1957) on the effectiveness of money as a motivator because, as he suggested, while the lack of it can cause dissatisfaction, its provision does not result in lasting satisfaction either.

Payment systems can indeed demotivate if they are badly conceived or administrated and result in inequitable rewards, which includes the failure to reward good performance adequately. And, because of all the other longer-term intrinsic motivating factors, it is undesirable to rely on money alone as *the* motivating factor.

Factors affecting satisfaction with the reward system

The following factors affecting satisfaction with the reward system need to be taken into account when formulating a reward philosophy:

- satisfaction with rewards is a function of what is expected as well as what is received;
- satisfaction is affected by comparison with other people in similar jobs and organizations;
- overall satisfaction is the result of a mix of rewards rather than any single reward.

As Beer (1984) writes:

> The evidence seems clear that intrinsic rewards and extrinsic rewards are both important and that they are not directly substitutable for each other. Employees who are well paid for repetitious, boring work will be dissatisfied with the lack of intrinsic rewards; just as employees paid poorly for interesting, challenging work may be dissatisfied with extrinsic rewards.

Beer also suggests that:

> Communication, participation and trust can have an important effect on people's perception of pay, the meaning they attach to a new pay

system, and their response to that system. In short, the *process may be as important as the system* (Beer's italics).

Contents of a reward philosophy

Every organization has to work out its own reward philosophy in the light of its analysis of business and individual needs. Philosophies are therefore contingent upon the organization's strategy, culture and values, and on the type of people it employs.

There is no such thing as a universal reward philosophy, but research carried out by the Top Pay Unit (1990) revealed the following recurrent themes.

■ reward policy is increasingly seen as a tool for bringing about cultural change within organizations;
■ much greater flexibility in reward systems is now required to enable employers to recruit and retain high-quality staff;
■ for managers and professional staff some link between pay and performance is increasingly taken for granted;
■ relating pay to performance increases the responsibilities of line managers who have to live with the consequences of their recommendations on rewards for their staff;
■ careful monitoring is necessary to ensure fairness and consistency in operating a reward system.

PAYING FOR PERFORMANCE

Arguments for paying for performance

There are many powerful arguments in favour of performance-related pay (PRP) or other types of incentive schemes. These include the following:

■ the best way to motivate people is to offer them more money;
■ PRP can help to develop a performance-oriented culture in an organization, by delivering a clear message that rewards are contingent on performance;
■ PRP and incentive schemes define expectations, focus effort and, if they are used as a basis for discussions between managers and their teams, increase commitment;
■ they serve to retain high-quality employees and deliver messages to poor quality employees either to improve or to go;
■ they are required simply because of market pressures and employee expectations that they will be part of competitive practice;
■ it is fundamentally equitable to reward people in accordance with their contribution.

Arguments against paying for performance

But there are also powerful arguments against paying for performance. These include the following:

- money is not the only motivator;
- it encourages 'short-termism' – going for the quick buck rather than the longer-term reward;
- attention is focused on volume and speed, not quality;
- intrinsic interest in a task – the sense that something is worth doing – declines when someone is given only external reasons for doing it;
- individual incentive schemes can damage teamwork;
- the criteria for success in an incentive scheme are very demanding and, if they are not met, a scheme is more likely to demotivate than motivate;
- it has never been proved that performance-related pay schemes do motivate on a consistent basis (so many other factors affect performance);
- the cost-effectiveness of many schemes is suspect – they can be costly to install and maintain, they cause wage drift (pay increasing without commensurate increases in productivity), and they can be a cause of endless dissatisfaction and strife.

Criteria for success

The five golden rules for a successful performance-related pay or incentive scheme are:

- individuals need to be clear about the targets and standards of performance required;
- it should be possible to measure performance against these targets and standards fairly and accurately;
- they must be in a position to influence their performance;
- there must be a clear link between performance and reward;
- the rewards must be meaningful enough to make the effort worth while.

These are demanding requirements and it is hardly surprising that pay for performance schemes are often introduced or maintained as an act of faith, and that the extent to which they give value for money is usually difficult to ascertain. Wright (1991) has stated that: 'Even the most ardent supporters of PRP recognize that it is extraordinarily difficult to manage well.'

Impact of payment for performance schemes

The disadvantages of PRP and incentive schemes, and the problems of developing and maintaining effective systems, have resulted in a reaction against the euphoria of the 1980s to a much more balanced approach in the 1990s. The IPM/NEDO research conducted in 1991 covered 40 British companies and came to the conclusion that in these organizations there had been insufficient clarity about the aims and objectives of PRP, that schemes had not been developed with sufficient rigour and fore-thought; that there was a notable absence in many organizations of any concern to set PRP in a wider context of performance management; and that more attention needed to be given to evaluation and monitoring.

PAYING FOR COMPETENCE

Bound up with the move to more performance based cultures is the realization that the traditional divide between the job and the job holder is becoming more tenuous. Jobs are shaped to a considerable extent by the way in which an individual performs them. The subtlety of this concept is not always captured well by systems which simply use job evaluation and grading definitions to define the post, and then add on performance pay arrangements to measure and reward the extent to which the post holder discharges his or her tasks and accountabilities. This is where a new approach to reward is needed.

Organizations need to design pay systems which focus on the value of the contribution of people in the context of their jobs and which can take account of the way an individual may modify his or her role and job content to fit their own skills, or in response to customer/market needs. What is defined within such pay systems is the role an individual performs – not a specific job. The role is expressed as a combination of broad accountabilities (a signpost of what is required to achieve organizational goals) and the competences (skills, experience, attitudes etc), which an individual may use to fulfil accountabilities.

PAYING FOR SKILL

Skills or knowledge-based pay schemes have been developed in response to the pressures for increasing the ability of employees to meet the greater level and range of skills required for the new technologies and working practices introduced by companies in recent years.

Skills-based schemes link pay to the acquisition of additional skills or knowledge. Employees are rewarded through direct payments for the ability to perform an operationally related range of tasks or skills, rather than for the actual work performed at any given time. Skills-based schemes determine the vertical rate of progression through grades as higher levels of skill are reached.

Skills-based schemes require the company to offer training for employees, to enable them to acquire new skills. This training is usually provided on a modular basis, ie training packages are developed which concentrate on a particular skill or group of skills (sometimes referred to as 'skill blocks').

Competitive advantage is achieved by having a skilled, flexible and committed labour force, and skills-based schemes have been developed to respond to this need. Such schemes do not exist simply to allow individual employees to pick up additional skills. Their purpose is, rather, to build and maintain a comprehensive mix of key skills over the whole workforce, in order to enhance flexibility, productivity and quality.

AN INTEGRATED APPROACH TO REWARD MANAGEMENT

An integrated approach to reward management will develop an appropriate mix of financial and non-financial rewards designed to increase extrinsic and intrinsic motivation.

Intrinsic motivation will be provided by job design, performance management and human resource development activities. The latter will focus on how managers can increase motivation and commitment by the ways in which they manage their staff. Although they should be responsible for managing financial rewards for their staff in accordance with company guidelines and budgets, they should be taught not to rely upon them – ultimately they will be held accountable for developing a skilled and well-motivated workforce.

Extrinsic motivation will also be provided for by the performance management system, which should be linked closely with any arrangements for performance-related pay.

Pay curve systems

A more flexible approach to financial reward which takes into account the key factors which should affect pay in a dynamic and competitive environment is provided by a pay curve system.

In this type of system, as developed by firms like Glaxo and Biocompatibles, pay is determined by an assessment of:

- an individual's competences;
- how effectively he or she uses those competences (performance);
- the value of those competences in the labour market.

Time is only a determinant of salary when it translates into skills or experience acquisition.

Pay curves are usually developed for job families, eg scientists, technicians, personnel. The operation of a pay curve system is illustrated in Figure 15.1.

Pay curves can play an important part in the development of integrated HRM systems because, not only can they relate pay to the development of competence through experience and training, but they can also define career curves which indicate how careers can develop as competence and performance levels increase.

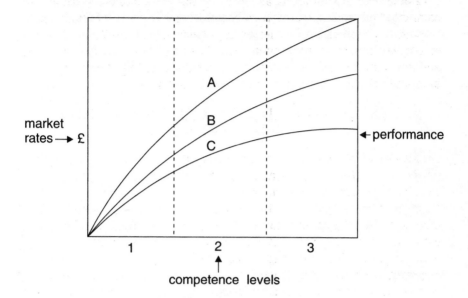

Figure 15.1 *A pay curve system*

THE ROLE OF THE HR SPECIALIST IN REWARD MANAGEMENT

HR specialists have a key role in developing and maintaining reward management systems. If an understanding of the factors affecting motivation and the various approaches to reward can be combined with an ability to analyze and diagnose both the needs of the organization and those of its workforce, then they can make a major contribution to the design of an integrated system.

They can and should ensure that a rigorous approach is adopted in defining aims. They can then see that the system is developed to meet those aims, and is consistent with the strategy and culture of the organization.

HR specialists can also provide an important input into design and maintenance by analyzing competence and skill levels, evaluating alternative schemes, linking PRP with a performance management system, tracking market rates, and monitoring and evaluating the impact of the system.

As facilitators and internal consultants, HR specialists can help management to implement change, and provide training and guidance to individual managers on the operation of the reward system. They will also, of course, be required to administer pay reviews and monitor the implementation of policies.

In an HRM setting, however, the real responsibility for running the reward system should rest with line managers. They should be given the maximum amount of authority to make reward decisions, although they will remain immediately responsible for operating in accordance with policy guidelines and within budgets. Managers are the people who are accountable for achieving results by making the best use of the resources available to them. They must, therefore, be given commensurate authority to manage one of the most important tools available to them, the reward system.

Chapter 16

HRM and Employee Relations

INTRODUCTION

HRM can be described as an approach used by companies to forge competitive advantage through their workforce. It is therefore concerned with all aspects of collective relationships, although HRM policies are often focused on individual employees. This chapter first summarizes the HRM approach to employee relations, and then examines the values underlying that approach. Consideration will be given in turn to the three main aspects of employee relations: industrial relations; communications; and worker involvement or participation.

THE HRM APPROACH TO EMPLOYEE RELATIONS

The essential features of the HRM approach are as follows.

- A belief that employees should be managed as efficiently and tightly as any other resource in order to maximize added value.
- A drive towards achieving competitive advantage by gaining commitment through intensive training and indoctrination programmes. This is coupled with a belief in the benefits of 'mutuality' – a shared interest in corporate success.
- The organization of complementary forms of communication, such as team briefing, alongside traditional collective bargaining – ie approaching employees directly as individuals or in groups, rather than through their representatives.
- The use of employee involvement techniques, such as quality circles or improvement groups.
- Continuous pressure on quality – total quality management.
- Increased flexibility in working arrangements to provide for the more cost-effective use of human resources.
- Emphasis on teamwork.
- A strategy of training employees in the particular package of skills appropriate to their own technologies, rather than buying in or

training skilled craft workers – this isolates employees, and so enhances their dependence on their employer.

The communication and involvement aspects of HRM are particularly important as they are directed at individual employees and could be regarded as an attempt to bypass or even marginalize the trade unions.

HRM VALUES AND EMPLOYEE RELATIONS

It has been suggested by Guest (1991) that:

Debates on pluralism, tripartism and trade union power ... no longer dominate our thinking and research. Instead, it is possible to detect a new orthodoxy under the optimistic but ambiguous label of human resource management.

HRM philosophy is optimistic because it echoes Peters and Austin's (1985) joyful words:

Trust people and treat them like adults, enthuse them by lively and imaginative leadership, develop and demonstrate an obsession for quality, make them feel they own the business, and your workforce will respond with total commitment.

This is inspiring stuff but as Guest (1991) has also commented, there is no clear link between commitment and performance.

HRM is ambiguous because, although its values favour creating what Handy (1989) calls 'a culture of consent', managements adopting an HRM approach could be said to be in the business of '*manufacturing* consent'; of using their power and their command of communications media to pressurize employees into accepting their (management's) values.

Ambiguity also exists because HRM values are unitarist, in that they assume the interests of management and employees coincide. But it can be argued that, however desirable a unitarist climate is from management's point of view, most UK organizations will be pluralist in the sense that they contain many separate, although related, interests. Trade union members in the company could be more committed to their union than to furthering the company's aims, although this does not mean they will be less productive.

HRM AND THE TRADE UNIONS

The unitarist perspective of HRM is regarded with suspicion by many trade unionists who see it as a strategy for reducing their influence, if not for eliminating them. Guest (1989b) has suggested that HRM is not necessarily anti-union, but it does present a threat in three ways.

1   HRM goals may be pursued through policies which bypass the union.

2   By practising high-quality management (which is what HRM demands), the need for the union as a protective device is likely to be reduced.

3   There is the risk that, in green-field sites or non-union plants, HRM policies could obviate the felt need for a union.

It is interesting to note, however, that when opening plants in green-field sites in the UK, Japanese companies like Nissan have accepted a trade union, and also instituted HRM practices such as flexibility and direct communication. But they have generally negotiated 'new style', single union agreements as described below which, while they recognize the right of employees to be represented by the union, preserve management's right to operate flexibly.

There seems to be no reason why an HRM approach cannot work well in a unionized plant. This is certainly the author's experience in Book Club Associates, where a 250-strong SOGAT 'chapel' in the distribution centre happily accepted flexibility and team briefing, although they drew the line at quality circles.

Single union agreements

Single union agreements, or 'new style' agreements as they were termed in the 1980s, are an option for any employer who does not wish to be plagued with a multi-union situation. They are particularly interesting for employers moving to a green-field site.

Nissan and Pirelli General provide good examples of firms with single union agreements. In the former case, the personnel director, Peter Wickens (1987), said that 'We considered the alternative of no trade unions and a multiplicity of trade unions. We rejected the first because it would lead to several years of counter-productive antagonism, and the latter because sooner or later it would lead to an erosion of our flexibility and single status objectives.' When Pirelli opened a factory in South Wales it was thought that the company might have to concede recognition to more than one union, unless it took action to avoid this undesirable situation by inviting a number of unions to submit proposals for them to be the sole union to represent employees.

Aims of single union agreements

The aims of employers in seeking single union agreements are to:

- eliminate the problems caused by inter-union disputes;
- have a focal point of contact as a stable basis for maintaining good relationships with the union;

- enable the company to select the union which would seem to be most appropriate;
- promote flexibility;
- reduce, if not eliminate, industrial strife.

These aims are very much in line with HRM philosophy and, in a unionized firm, or one that is prepared to recognize a union, single union deals can play an important part in developing an integrated approach to human resource management which supports other initiatives concerning commitment, flexibility, skills development and performance improvement.

Features of single union deals

There is no typical single union deal, but some or all of the following features may be included.

1   *Single status* – all conditions the same, except salary.

2   *Community of interests or mutuality* – explicit statements may be included in the agreement to the effect that the well-being of employees is dependent upon the company's success.

3   *Involvement* – the company accepts that employees have a genuine 'say' in terms of consultation and advice, and the company will also be willing to disclose the necessary information.

4   *Flexibility* – flexibility is an accepted method of working, particularly in high-tech companies, but this requires effort on the part of the company to train and retrain staff.

5   *Inexhaustible disputes procedure* – this overcomes the inherent problems of normal disputes procedures, which, although they may include a peace clause restraining the parties from taking industrial action while the matter is 'in procedure', specifically or implicitly allow for the procedure to become exhausted without the dispute being resolved. A single union agreement may be 'inexhaustible' in that the compulsory final stage of pendulum arbitration provides for a binding solution to the dispute. However, this does not apply to all such deals and a comprehensively-worded peace clause may still be included.

6   *Unnecessary strikes* – the aim of a new style agreement is to make strikes unnecessary. It does not usually attempt to outlaw strikes because of the contractual complications of making such agreements legally enforceable. As a strike substitute, the final offer agreement can threaten to impose an unacceptable penalty (the other party's offer) if agreement is not reached, and risk-averse negotiators prefer to avoid this outcome.

7 *Responsible negotiation* – conventional negotiations are subject to what have been termed 'narcotic' or 'chilling' effects. The narcotic effect happens when there is compulsory arbitration and negotiators are in danger of turning to it as an easy and habit-forming release from the obligation to conduct hard, responsible negotiations. The chilling effect on the parties' determination to reach agreement occurs when they know a normal 'split the difference' type of arbitration may happen at the last stage, and there is therefore an incentive to maintain excessive demands. Final offer arbitration is designed to avoid these effects. The parties have an incentive not to hold everything back for the arbitration and it is hoped that the final offers will be sufficiently close together to be accepted by the losing party.

An example of a single union agreement

The Pirelli agreement of 1987 with the Managerial, Administrative and Technical and Supervisors' Association (MATSA) of the GMB, as described by Yeandle and Clark (1989), stated that the general aim of the agreement was to 'ensure the operational and commercial success of the unit to the mutual benefit of the company and its employees and to bind and commit the signatories to this aim'.

The following principles were agreed:

■ employee commitment to and identification with the achievement of the unit's operational objectives;
■ single trade union recognition and single staff status to include common conditions of employment, and an integrated salary structure;
■ acceptance of industrial and employee relations policies and attitudes which will foster employee cooperation, communication and involvement, and preclude industrial action.

Perhaps the most innovative aspects of the particular agreement were the four operational commitments.

1 A clear commitment to complete employee flexibility, so that employees may be allocated any tasks or duties which are required (subject to duties being within their capability and to appropriate training).

2 Both the union and the employers agree not to apply any restrictions or delays to the fully effective implementation of the unit's operational requirements.

3 The union is committed to the achievement and maintenance of high-quality standards of work and a speedy response to customer requirements.

4   The union agrees to cooperate actively with the introduction of change, whether in products, materials, techniques or working practices.

5   Employees must be willing to undertake training and be trained, as required.

6   The management is obliged to provide appropriate training, materials and equipment to enable employees to achieve high-quality standards of work and high levels of job satisfaction.

Advantages of single union agreements

- *For the employer* – flexibility, an end to demarcation, machinery to solve disputes without loss of production, a better-trained, motivated and involved workforce, and the opportunity of ending confrontational industrial relations.
- *For the trade union* – the opportunity for harmonization, greater industrial democracy, improved public image, increased membership, recognition in areas that might otherwise become non-union, the ability to resolve disputes without loss of pay or union funds, better job prospects because of increased productivity, better training for its members which increases their ability to 'sell their skills' on the job market.

Disadvantages

From the employer's point of view, a potential disadvantage is that they might appear to be putting all their eggs into one basket. There could be problems if relationships were to deteriorate. But it is up to employers to create conditions where such breakdowns do not occur. Single union deals do demand high levels of competence from management, a willingness to invest in training and a genuine desire to involve their workforce in decision making.

As some unions see it, these agreements are suspect because they remove their major weapon – the strike – and the TUC has recommended that unions should not sign any clause which removes their right to take industrial action. But this does not apply to arbitration clauses, which can be triggered voluntarily or by mutual agreement. Some trade unionists feel that they could give away more than they gain if they conclude a single union deal.

Single union deals, with many of the characteristics mentioned above, have been signed by a number of unions, including the maverick EPTU, AEU, GMB and TGWU. They are not, however, a major feature of the UK industrial relations scene yet and the number of new deals being negotiated is fairly small.

Single union deals offer advantages to both employers and trade unions, but they are hard work, both to negotiate and maintain. However, they are the way forward for firms on green-field sites or those who are determined to achieve greater flexibility and to minimize strife in the workplace.

COMMUNICATIONS

Organizations function by means of the collective action of people, yet each individual is capable of taking independent action, which may not be in line with policy or instructions, or may not be reported properly to other people who ought to know about it. Good communications are required to achieve coordinated results.

Organizations are subject to the influence of continuous change which affects the work employees do, their well-being and their security. Change can be managed only by ensuring that the reasons for an implication of change are communicated to those affected, in terms which they can understand and accept.

Individuals are motivated by the extrinsic reward system and the intrinsic rewards coming from the work itself. But the degree to which they are motivated depends upon the amount of responsibility and scope for achievement provided by their job, and upon their expectations that the rewards they will get will be the ones they want, and will follow from the efforts they make. Feelings about work and the associated rewards depend very much on the effectiveness of communications from their boss and within the company.

Above all, good two-way communications are required so that management can keep employees informed of the policies and plans affecting them, and employees can react promptly with their views about management's proposals and actions. Change cannot be managed properly without an understanding of the feelings of those affected by it, and an efficient system of communications is needed to understand and influence these feelings.

But the extent to which good communications create satisfactory relationships, rather than simply reducing unsatisfactory ones, can be exaggerated. A feature of management practices during the 20th century is the way in which different management theories become fashionable or influential for a while and then decline in favour. Among these has been the 'good communications' theory of management. This approach to dealing with management problems is based upon the following assumptions.

1   The needs and aims of both employees and management are, in the long run, the same in any organization. Managers' and employees' ideas and objectives can all be fitted together to form a single conceptual framework.

2   Any differences in opinion between management and employees are due to misunderstandings which have arisen because communications are not good enough.

3   The solution to industrial strife is to improve communications.

This theory is attractive and has some validity. Its weakness is that the assumptions are too sweeping, particularly the assumption that the ultimate objectives of management and workers are necessarily identical. The good communications theory, like paternalism, seems to imply that a company can develop loyalty, by keeping people informed and treating them well. But people working in organizations have other and, to them, more important loyalties elsewhere – and why not?

The existence of different loyalties and points of view in an organization does not mean that communication is unimportant. If anything, the need for a good communications system becomes even greater when differences and conflict exist. But it can only alleviate those differences and pave the way to better cooperation. It cannot solve them.

It is therefore necessary to bear in mind that the group with which we identify – the reference group – influences our attitudes and feelings. 'Management' and 'the union', as well as our family, our ethnic background, our political party and our religious beliefs (if any) constitute a reference group and colour our reactions to information. What each group 'hears' depends on its own interests. Shared experiences and common frames of reference have much more influence than exhortations from management. These come from people with whom employees may feel they have nothing in common, especially if the messages contain information which conflicts with what they already believe.

What management should say

What management wants to say depends upon an assessment of what employees need to know which, in turn, is affected by what they want to hear.

Management aims to achieve three things: first, to get employees to understand and accept what management proposes to do in areas affecting them; secondly, to get employees to act in the way management wants; and, thirdly, to get employees to identify themselves more closely with the company and its achievements.

Communication systems

The media that are available for communications include magazines, newsletters, bulletins, notice boards and videos. But the aim should be to achieve two-way communications, so that management can obtain feedback on its plans. Team briefing is a system which can help to achieve this aim.

Team briefing

Team briefing involves everyone in an organization, level by level, in face-to-face meetings, to present, receive and discuss information. Team briefing aims to overcome the gaps and inadequacies of casual briefing by injecting some order into the system.

Team briefing should operate in the following way.

Organization

- Covers all levels in an organization.
- Fewest possible steps between the top and bottom.
- Between 4 and 18 in each group.
- Run by the immediate leader of each group at each level (who must be properly trained and briefed).

Subjects

- Policies – explanations of new or changed policies.
- Plans – as they affect the organization as a whole and the immediate group.
- Progress – how the organization and the group is getting on; what the latter needs to do to improve.
- People, new appointments, points about personal matters (pay, security, procedures).

Timing and duration

- Ideally once a month for those in charge of others and once every two months for every individual in the organization – but teams should meet only if there is something to say.
- Duration not longer than 20 to 30 minutes.

The merit of team briefing is that it enables face-to-face communications to be planned and, to a reasonable degree, formalized. It is easy, however, for it to start on a wave of enthusiasm, and then to wither away because of lack of sufficient drive and enthusiasm from the top downward, inadequately trained and motivated managers (as is the case with many HRM initiatives, especially in the field of communication, middle managers can make or break the process), reluctance of management to allow subjects of real importance to be discussed throughout the system, and insufficient feedback upwards through each level.

A team briefing system must be led and controlled effectively from the top, but it does require a senior manager with specific responsibility to advise on the subject matter and the preparation of briefs (it is important to have well-prepared material to ensure that briefing is carried out consistently and thoroughly at each level), to train managers and supervisors, and to monitor the system by checking on the effectiveness and frequency of meetings.

PARTICIPATION

What is participation?

Participation takes place when management and employees are jointly involved in making decisions on matters of mutual interest, where the aim is to produce solutions to the problems which will benefit all concerned. Participation does not mean that the parties subordinate their own interests entirely. But it does mean that they aim to achieve objectives which are not in fundamental conflict with those of the other party, and which can, therefore, be integrated to some degree. Participation does not require total and bland agreement all the time, and bargaining about issues is not excluded. It is akin to integrative or cooperative bargaining, in which parties find common or complementary interests and solve problems confronting both of them.

Participation should be distinguished from negotiation which, although it involves joint decision making, does this by a process of distributive or conjunctive bargaining, where the sole aim is to resolve pure conflicts of interest.

Levels of participation

Participation takes place at the following levels in an enterprise:

- job level;
- management level;
- policy-making level;
- ownership level.

Participation at the job level involves the team leader and his or her immediate group, and the processes include the communication of information about the work, the delegation of authority and the interchange of ideas about how the work should be done. These processes are essentially informal.

Participation at management level can involve sharing information and decision making about issues which affect the way in which work is planned, coordinated and controlled, and the conditions under which the work is carried out. There are limitations. Management as a whole, and individual managers, must retain the authority to do what their function requires. Participation does not imply anarchy. But it does require some degree of willingness on the part of management to share its decision-making powers. At this level, participation becomes more formalized, through consultative committees, briefing groups or other joint bodies involving management and trade unionists.

At the policy-making level, where the direction in which the business is going is determined, total participation implies sharing the power to make the key decisions on investments, disinvestments, new ventures, expansions and retractions which affect the future well-being of both the company and its employees. Ultimately, it means that such decisions are made fairly by directors who represent the interests of the owners, the management and the work people. The proposal to have a supervisory board upon which worker representatives have the power to veto major investment decisions, mergers or takeovers, and closures or major redeployment, is not full participation. However, it is in accordance with the reality of the divided loyalties that worker representatives would have if they had to share the responsibility for unpopular decisions by becoming full board members in the accepted sense.

At the ownership level, participation may imply a share in the equity, which is not meaningful unless the workers have sufficient control, through voting rights, to determine the composition of the board. Workers' cooperatives are also participative in the sense that the workers, including managers and supervisors, *are* the management and must therefore be involved in joint decision making at board level.

Mechanisms for participation

At the job level, participation should be as informal as possible. Groups may be called together on an *ad hoc* basis to consider a particular problem, but formal committees should be avoided in small departments (say, fewer than 250 people) or at section level. Team briefing can be used to provide for informal two-way communications. However, more formality may be appropriate in larger organizations where there is scope for the use of joint consultative committees or joint negotiating committees with carefully defined terms of reference on the matters they can discuss.

At the policy-forming level, participation becomes more difficult to organize. This is when management is most reluctant to abandon its prerogatives unless forced to by legislation. Unions, as already mentioned, do not like to be put in a position where they may have to endorse unpopular decisions. A works council may be given the chance to discuss policy issues, but if the final decision on any matter which is clearly not negotiable is made at board level, it may be seen as an ineffectual body.

Another important form of participation and involvement, which is often used in an HRM setting, is the quality circle, sometimes known as an improvement group.

Quality circles

Quality circles are small groups of volunteers who are engaged in related work, and who meet regularly to discuss and propose ways of improving working methods or arrangements under a trained leader.

Aims

The aims of quality circles are to:

- give those doing the job more scope to use their experience and know-how;
- provide opportunities to tap the knowledge of employees, who may know more about work problems which are hidden from more remote managers and supervisors;
- improve productivity and quality;
- improve employee relations;
- win commitment to the organization.

Essential features

The essential features of quality circles are that they:

- consist of volunteers;
- have a trained leader;
- hold regular meetings which are strictly limited in duration – often one hour.

Prerequisites for success

- *Management support* – the first prerequisite is that top management believes in the value of quality circles and is committed to their success. Middle management and supervision must also be involved in their introduction. They are the people who are most likely to have reservations about quality circles because they can see them as a threat to their authority and reputation – for example, when a problem is overcome by a circle rather than by the supervisor. Without management support, quality circles die, as they often do.
- *Trade unions* – trade unions should also be informed of the plan to introduce quality circles. Some unions are hostile because they feel that quality circles can reduce their influence and power, and that management is deliberately introducing them for this purpose.
- *Facilitator* – the introduction and maintenance of a quality circle needs a 'facilitator' who trains, encourages and guides quality circle members, ensures that they are given the resources they need and sets up presentation sessions. The facilitator is often a line manager rather than a personnel officer or a trainer. This vital role also involves encouraging the circles and ensuring that top management backing continues by keeping them informed of the benefits provided by quality circles – publicity on their achievements is important. The facilitator can also deal with any problems quality circles meet in getting information or in dealing with management.

- *Training* – training is an important part of the quality circle. Team leaders need an initial two to three-day training course in the analytical techniques they will use, and in team building and presentation skills. They also need refresher training from time to time. Team leaders, with the help of facilitators, also train the members of their team. This training effort is a valuable spin-off from a quality circle programme. Instruction in leadership, problem solving and analytical skills is a useful way of developing existing or potential supervisors. Membership of a quality circle is also a means of developing skills, as well as getting more involved.

ROLE OF THE HR SPECIALIST IN EMPLOYEE RELATIONS

In many organizations in the recent past, personnel directors and managers devoted a large proportion of their time to industrial relations. Line managers tended to leave it to the experts to deal with HR problems and to negotiate with the unions.

HRM takes that responsibility away from the personnel or industrial relations department and places it firmly where it belongs, in the hands of line management. It is up to them to build and maintain good relationships with their staff. They cannot shift that responsibility to anyone else. Many industrial relations problems in the past have occurred because line management failed to take enough interest in relationships with employees, until it was too late.

HR specialists, however, still have an important role to play in employee relations. They can advise management on industrial relations strategy, legal requirements and trade union agreements. They can help to develop tactics for dealing with negotiations based upon their understanding of the issues – which they should take pains to acquire. They can also act as a bridge between management and trade union officials, because they can convey messages and test reactions without committing either side (if they are not involved in the actual negotiation).

HR specialists can also administer communication systems and facilitate quality circles. Without their encouragement and help these methods of communication and involvement can all too easily wither and die.

Chapter 17

Implementing HRM

INTRODUCTION

HRM is a philosophy which provides guidance on how management should exercise its responsibility for managing people. But the study conducted by the Warwick University Industrial Relations Research Unit (Storey 1992) as summarised on page 212, my own research (Armstrong 1987) and other analyses of HRM in practice have indicated that, while HRM as a concept may have gained some credibility, it tends to be introduced incrementally and often in a fragmented way.

In theory, HRM is implemented by adopting a strategic approach to the development of a mutually reinforcing range of personnel policies and processes. A human resource management system, according to this prescription, should operate within a conceptual framework which enables a coherent set of policy goals and methods of implementing them to be established.

But it is not possible to prescribe the nature of that framework. The HRM concept is too generalized to provide instant remedies in the shape of ready-made answers as to what should be done, how it should be done or when it should be done. HRM cannot be presented in the form of a universal process for improving the way in which people are managed in organizations.

All that can be suggested is that there are a certain number of aspects of HRM philosophy which should be considered by an organization when it is developing its processes for managing people. These include:

- strategic integration – of HRM and business strategies;
- the will to develop an internally cohesive approach which aligns the key human resource initiatives of resourcing, development, performance management and reward so that together they can make a strong contribution to the achievement of organizational effectiveness and competitive advantage;
- a conviction that culture management is important;
- a marked shift from, as Storey (1989) puts it, 'merely securing compliance to the more ambitious one of winning commitment';
- a profound belief that the employee resource is worth investing in;

- the recognition that the organization must operate more flexibly in the face of global competition and change;
- the active pursuit of total quality;
- a strong emphasis on the communication of management's plans and values to the workforce;
- a drive to achieve partnership with trade unions which recognizes their respective interests but stresses the importance of working together to achieve mutual benefits.

These assumptions and beliefs provide the basis for much of the rhetoric which surrounds HRM. But to what extent are they being put into practice, and if so, how? In the next section of this chapter I describe how a number of organizations have introduced HRM approaches, including my own attempt to do this at Book Club Associates.

PUTTING HRM INTO PRACTICE

Research in twenty major companies in the UK on what they were doing about HRM (Armstrong 1989a) revealed that the personnel directors of such organizations as BAT, Cadbury Schweppes, Ford, IBM, ICL, the International Stock Exchange, Legal and General, the MB (Metal Box) Group, The National Health Service, Nissan, W H Smith, Thorn EMI, Unilever and The Wellcome Foundation had observed the same trends towards the implementation of an HRM approach. These were: an emphasis on strategy, human resource management being concerned with cultural change and empowering people, the importance of resourcing and the stress on performance, quality and customer care. But the companies went about it in different ways. Some examples are given below from this research together with a description of the experience of introducing HRM at Book Club Associates.

The MB Group

The MB Group's campaign for change was based on:

- a shared agenda against which progress can be measured;
- a communication programme aimed at internal and external audiences;
- an increased investment in training so that managers develop both the skills and the vision to manage the change process.

The top management philosophy underpinning this initiative was as follows:

It is proposed to run a broad campaign across Metal Box for a broad programme of change, rather than to tackle each change objective in a piecemeal way. External experience, increasingly reported by industrialists, consultants and academics, leads strongly to the view that the bolder and more visionary the agenda set by top management, the more effective and faster are the results achieved. If employees at all levels can be convinced that radical change is being adopted across the range of the company's activities and is directed towards major improvements in overall performance (and thereby to continued investment and greater job security and satisfaction), they are more likely to support a 'hearts and minds campaign' and change their own behaviour.

Thorn EMI

At Thorn EMI the thrust was towards strategic integration which started from a top management analysis (facilitated by the group personnel director) of the main characteristics of the group. These were:

- the capacity to manage its businesses in different national markets and to exploit its creative/marketing, technological and management skills internationally;
- its ability to give real opportunity and authority for strong managers to be enterprising in their own businesses;
- its ability to coordinate its approaches fast and responsively to market opportunities which require integrated action by more than one business area;
- having a strong balance between demanding excellence of performance from its managers and investing humanity, skill and time into helping managers to improve their performance and potential;
- its ability to manage its research and technologies in a market-sensitive manner.

This analysis provided the basis for determining strategic priorities for the development of an organization which would manifest these characteristics.

Cadbury Schweppes

At Cadbury Schweppes a major thrust in their human resource policies in the late 1980s was in the field of participation. A project group on the implications of change produced this statement on the aims of the programme:

The following objectives are those affecting the area of employee involvement which will enable Cadbury Schweppes to meet the challenges of the future.

1   To produce the highest quality product at the lowest cost in line with changing business and market conditions and ensuring a continuing competitive advantage.

2   To explore, evaluate and capitalize each distribution opportunity while continuing to operate in the most cost-effective system to sustain long-term growth.

3   To develop the employee business link through the establishment of open communication systems that ensure employees understand and are committed to business goals and performance.

4   To create and maintain an environment which develops and nurtures long-term employee commitment.

5   To develop an organization which encourages a participative management style.

6   To review and critically evaluate all of the traditional conditions of employment and management practices, modifying those as required to achieve high-quality results.

7   To provide direction and support to employee groups that enables those groups to initiate, adapt and accept new ideas and technology for continued profitable business growth.

8   To develop a management profile which encourages a participative leadership style embracing the organization's values and continuing to improve overall company performance.

ICL

ICL based its programme of HRM development in the 1980s on its key business strategies which were built around:

- high-value solutions to defined markets;
- commitment to open systems – providing customers with greater flexibility in the choice of manufacturer and with confidence for the future;
- collaborations – to gain market or technical leverage;
- organizational responsiveness – to react to the fast-changing market;
- focus on systems and solutions for customers and on providing real added value for them in running their business.

The starting point was a statement of the following seven commitments.

1   *Commitment to change*   Success in our company now depends on each individual's willingness to accept change as something valuable, something to be welcomed, something to be responded to with energy and resourcefulness. Our business *is* change.

2   *Commitment to customers*   The overriding importance of the needs and expectations of our customers should condition all our thinking and govern all our planning. We are now a business driven by the business needs of our market.

3   *Commitment to excellence*   ICL's sights are now set on world success. That demands excellence in everything we undertake. And excellence will be achieved only by adopting 'can do' attitudes and the highest levels of cooperation and teamwork throughout the company.

4   *Commitment to teamwork*   Effective teamwork produces results far superior to anything the individuals could achieve working in isolation. To secure this $1 + 1 = 3$ return, our teamwork must be based on the need to heighten the capabilities, competence and contribution of each individual.

5   *Commitment to achievement*   ICL is an achievement company. Recognition, rewards, promotion and opportunities for career and job development depend absolutely on results delivered.

6   *Commitment to people development*   We are a people company. Our main strength lies in the quality and skill of the people who work here. Real progress will come about only by constantly developing and improving our skills. Development of this kind – people development – is one of the basic requirements for business success.

7   *Commitment to creating a productivity showcase   All* our systems, *all* aspects of our performance should be of 'showcase' standard – a standard which gives customers something to strive for.

These commitments were followed through initially by an extended core education programme. Major shifts were needed in the way people thought, made their decisions and conducted their lives in the company. Some of them can be summarized as follows:

FROM		TO
technology-led	→	marketing-led
tactical and short term	→	strategic, long term
internal focus	→	external focus
try and do everything	→	specialized target markets
parochial	→	company commitments
procedure-bound	→	innovative and open-minded
UK expert	→	global competitor

This programme continued with the introduction of a mix of people management processes which included performance management as a pivotal element. As described by Williams (1991):

Each of these initiatives was a vital ingredient in its own right but it was their collective effect on winning the 'hearts and minds' of ICL's managers and employees that proved to be of crucial importance.

The performance management system consisted of a logical cycle of four steps linked with the company's business strategies.

- *Step 1* – The determination and *setting of individual objectives* which support the achievement of the over-all business strategies
- *Step 2* – A *formal appraisal* centred on what was achieved against these pre-agreed objectives. This results in the joint determination of a personal/job improvement plan, a career development plan and a training plan, plus the allocation of a performance rating by the manager
- *Step 3* – A separate *pay review* in which the level of pay increase is based largely on the actual level of achievement made against the pre-agreed objectives.
- *Step 4* – An *organization capability review* which, as part of the normal business review process, focuses on the total organizational capability of each part of the organization to achieve the future business strategies.

ICL's approach to developing people and their potential as described by Beattie and Tampoe (1990) was to

- know what the aiming point for individual careers is, ie the next step on their career ladder;
- plan 'building blocks' of experience constantly to add value; this means defining skill and experience profiles for managers;
- plan the use of training, making sure that it can be used quickly in real life;
- set up growth opportunities within the job, exposing people to new areas;
- identify and use 'development positions' – positions where good people can make an early contribution without specialist prior knowledge;
- provide international exposure;
- emphasize that career management is a mutual responsibility between the company and the individual.

Book Club Associates

Book Club Associates is a young, highly successful firm which is a dominant force in its market. Its success can be largely attributed to its culture, values, management style and the fact that it has made good use of its knowledge base and the specialized skills it has developed. The culture is market and customer service oriented. All the chief executives since the company was founded twenty-five years ago have had a background in marketing. Suitable adjectives with which to describe the way things are done in BCA are opportunistic, entrepreneurial, dynamic and informal. It believes in achieving a high degree of professionalism in the things which count – marketing and the provision and management of its key resources – finance, operational systems, information technology and people. The climate is friendly. There are, of course, disagreements on business matters, but they are dealt with openly and not on a personal basis.

Management style is informal with a tendency towards the autocratic – a function of the type of business, where quick reactions and fast decisions must be a way of life. Informal channels of communications worked well, but BCA had not been particularly good at developing formal systems. Integration, when there are many entrepreneurs about, is a problem.

The starting point

The starting point was in the late 1970s when, with outside help, an organization development study was carried out. This diagnostic review revealed that the company's strengths were a skilled and enthusiastic workforce which was highly committed and identified with BCA, a climate and style conducive to teamwork and an emphasis on innovation and development. The weaknesses were a lack of clarity over roles, undue overlap between functions, poor communications and growing signs of stress.

By the mid 1980s BCA had gone some way towards the development of a human resource management system. HRM was defined in the BCA context as a total approach to the strategic management of a key resource which was the responsibility of the board and had to be implemented by line management. The role of the personnel function was to provide advice and support in the implementation of HRM.

The strategies which emerged from this analysis were to

- develop more integration of activities through project teams;
- achieve flexibility in response to change;
- develop a climate of cooperation and trust;
- achieve an appropriate balance between the flexible and informal approach necessary in a rapidly developing and innovative organization and the need to formalize systems and processes as the business grew in size and complexity;
- create career management procedures to maximize potential, identify career paths and deal with problems.

These strategies were broad, but they provided a good starting point for the development of an HRM approach. This has made good progress but there is still a lot to do; which goes to show that even with top management enthusiasm and commitment, the installation of HRM can take time. It is, in fact, a process that will never be completed – times change and so does HRM.

The process

The member of the executive board responsible for human resources was expected, like his colleagues, to play a full part in formulating corporate strategies and participating in the development of the business. His specific brief was to examine the implications of proposed strategies from the organizational point of view, making sure that the right calibre people were available to innovate, to develop and generally to take the business forward. And in defining and getting what was required, an important aim was to ensure a good fit between the individual and the organizational culture.

The strategic base

The foundation for HRM strategies was developed by management at a series of residential workshops – a regular feature in BCA. These produced the following combined mission and value statement.

■ Book Club Associates is in the business of the direct marketing and supply of in-house leisure products for the purposes of entertainment, education and self-improvement.

■ BCA earns its living in a competitive world, and it needs to compete successfully to meet its obligations to all those who have a stake in the business – its owners, its members and the people who work there.

■ The basis of our enterprise is the goodwill of our customers – the members who join our book clubs and those who buy from our catalogues. We are in business to identify and meet their needs.

■ The success of BCA ultimately depends upon the quality and commitment of its people. BCA believes in providing individuals with opportunities to make the best of their abilities and to grow with the firm. We also believe that openness, trust and fair treatment together form the basis of the good working relationships upon which the effectiveness of the organization depends.

Strategic planning was carried out on top-down, bottom-up basis. That is, top management provided the parameters on growth and profitability targets and key ratios, while senior and middle managers prepared proposals for top management consideration. The board spent two 'away days' developing broad strategies, which were then discussed with the fifty most senior managers at a one and a half day's corporate planning conference. The HR director managed this process. He was also responsible alongside members of the personnel function for formulating the HR strategy as part of the total business strategy.

The human resource plan was set out under three major headings:

■ *People* – improving quality, developing potential.
■ *Performance* – increasing the accountability of managers for results, relating pay more specifically to performance, increasing commitment by better communications and more involvement.

■ *Productivity* – analyzing the use of human resources throughout the organization so that planned growth was achieved with lower costs per unit of output.

This plan was translated into a number of programmes which were initiated and monitored by the board in its capacity as the body which had the overall responsibility for human resource management. The programmes were implemented by line management and the personnel department, which was there to provide the professional expertise and resources needed by the board and managers generally.

The people programmes included an analysis of the longer-term organizational requirements which emerged from the corporate plan and the search – inside and out – for staff with the particular qualifications and expertise needed. The career development programme looked more systematically at what employees needed to know and do to succeed as part of BCA's future.

They also included the introduction of a performance management system and the complete revision of the pay structure to provide for performance related pay at all levels.

A particularly important part of the HRM programme was the introduction of team briefing and quality circles. The latter were started in all parts of the organization except in the distribution centre where the trade union refused to cooperate (they did, however, accept team briefing).

The whole programme was backed up by a system of performance related training and career development.

These initiatives were, of course, taken progressively and took over three years to introduce. Priority was given to the performance management system and the associated performance related training programmes. These were supported by the communications exercise. The resourcing, training and career development aspects were developed on a continuing basis but, reluctantly, innovations in these areas had to be delayed while what were regarded as the essential foundations of the HRM system (performance and reward management) were built.

Culture management

The approach to culture management at Book Club Associates was to preserve what was good about the culture and not to indulge in change for change's sake. This meant deliberately promoting a climate of enterprise, endeavour and informality, resisting pressures for excessive bureaucracy, flattening the organization structure to compress hierarchies and continuing to encourage a joint approach to planning and problem-solving. This was done by senior management setting an example, by specific organizational methods, including the extensive use of project teams, and by group training designed to develop skills in working with and leading teams.

The continuous analysis of the impact of the culture on organizational behaviour was used as the basis for planning change programmes by opening up communications and achieving more participation through quality circles and other means.

Key factors

The creation of an HRM culture at Book Club Associates was helped by the existence of a strong and successful culture, powerful chief executives who meant what they said when they stated that BCA's most valuable asset was people and the determination of the HR director to make progress. It was also dependent on getting priorities right.

The introduction of new HRM policies and practices had to be phased in to avoid swamping line management, who were also liable to say that 'we have our own jobs to do and cannot spare time for all this HRM stuff'. In fact, the biggest potential obstacle to progress was the attitude of middle managers and supervisors who were themselves under threat because of the delayering exercise. It is essential to carry them with you when developing HRM, and this is not easy.

THE APPROACH TO IMPLEMENTING HRM

It is noticeable that the well-known 'HRM' companies such as IBM, Digital, Hewlett-Packard, Motorola, Nissan and Texas Instruments are large, multinational, single product-range firms which have a tradition of sophisticated personnel practices and a belief in the importance of treating people as valued assets. An HRM approach is less likely to be adopted in a highly diversified conglomerate, especially a 'financial control' company as described by Goold and Campbell (1986).

Smaller firms such as Book Club Associates can introduce HRM but they are likely already to have a well-developed culture, strong leadership and a powerful personnel function.

Research conducted by Guest (1989b) and Hendry and Pettigrew (1990) indicated that the introduction of HRM in British firms is often a slow and difficult process and because of this is not particularly widespread. Certainly, the author's own experience at Book Club Associates is that it took several years to make a significant impact.

The Warwick University Industrial Relations Research Unit Study

More recent information on HRM in action was provided by a Warwick University Industrial Relations Research Unit study as described by Storey (1992). This consisted of an examination of how key HRM characteristics were being applied in fifteen major British organizations including Austin Rover, British Rail, Bradford Council, the NHS, Smith and Nephew and Whitbread. The dimensions were those listed in Table 3.2 of this book (page 37). The analysis compared current developments in HRM with the basic 1970s recipe for good personnel and industrial relations practice, which was built around standardization and procedures as expressed, for example, in job evaluation, agreed trade union facilities and the like.

The main finding of the study was that there had been an extensive take up of HRM style approaches in these British mainstream organizations. However, there was no evidence that an entirely unitarist approach to industrial relations was being adopted, although there was a shift away from the proceduralist recipe – eleven of the fifteen companies expressed impatience with rules.

Most of the cases failed to show much in the way of an integrated approach to employee practices management and there was little evidence of strategic integration with the corporate plan. As Storey writes:

> This finding lends some support to the view that the 'HRM model' is itself not a coherent, integrated phenomenon. Many of the initiatives recorded in the case research ... arise for diverse reasons, and in practice they shared little in common.

This, according to Storey, might indicate the true nature of HRM,

> ie that it is in reality a symbolic label behind which lurk multifarious practices, many of which are not mutually dependent on one another.

Other interesting findings from this research included the strong emphasis on 'business need' as the prime guide to action, the emergence of general 'business managers' and line managers as key players in employment issues, and the extent to which line managers as well as personnel directors were intent in stressing their engagement with 'culture change' activities.

No prescriptions for HRM

British research and experience has shown that it is pointless to prescribe any packaged approach to HRM. It depends entirely on the requirements of the organization, and these will be a function of its strategies, culture, structure, business environment, resources, processes and traditions. Every organization must do it in its own particular way. There is no such thing as a universal HRM prescription.

The conceptual framework of HRM does, however, provide a basis for reviewing and integrating current and proposed initiatives concerning people management in an organization. And it can help to develop a coherent view of HRM policy as a support to the achievement of the organization's strategies. But within that framework, an incremental approach is almost inevitable, except, possibly, when starting on a green field site like Nissan. ICL, for example, started with a culture change programme and then progressively introduced processes such as performance management, career development, total quality management and new systems of reward management.

An incremental approach may have to be adopted, but as each HRM process is developed and introduced, added value can be obtained if thought is given to how it reinforces and will be reinforced by the other HRM processes already in place or to be launched shortly. Overriding these initiatives, a continuing programme of communication, education and training can do much to help people accept the reason for change and to manage it effectively as it happens.

While there are no 'quick fixes' which can be applied to the development of an HRM approach, there are three areas to which it may be worth giving some consideration in order to provide guidance on the approaches that can be adopted. These are:

1　Creating the strategy;

2　Designing a mutually reinforcing and internally consistent set of HRM processes;

3　Defining the roles of those involved.

Creating the strategy

A strategy for developing HRM should ideally start from an analysis of the organization's current business strategies and its culture, processes, systems and structures. It may be appropriate to conduct this as a 'SWOT' analysis, considering in turn the organization's strengths, weaknesses, opportunities and threats.

This analysis leads to a diagnosis of the present state of the organization and a description of what needs to be done about it. The action programme refers to initiatives in the fields of organization restructuring, culture management, resourcing, human resource development and performance and reward management, and employee relations. The programme indicates priorities, timings, responsibilities and the resources required.

Designing a mutually reinforcing set of HRM processes

It is helpful in the first place to define the outcomes expected of an HRM development programme. The contribution of the various HRM inputs to achieving these outcomes can then be assessed.

Conceptually, this process can be carried out by using the matrix shown in Table 17.1. This indicates how different HRM inputs can be combined to contribute to the achievement of outcomes. It demonstrates the extent to which these inputs are mutually reinforcing.

Table 17.1 *HRM inputs and outcomes*

| | | HRM outcomes | | | | | | |
		performance	quality	skills acquisition and development	motivation	commitment	teamwork	flexibility
HRM inputs	Organization	★					★	★
	Resourcing	★	★	★				
	HRD	★	★	★	★	★	★	★
	Performance management	★	★	★	★	★	★	
	Reward management	★			★			
	Communications	★	★			★		
	Participation	★	★			★	★	
	Industrial relations	★						★

The links between the key HRM activities and the fundamental process of strategy formulation are shown in Figure 17.1. This illustrates the following points which are relevant when developing an internally consistent and mutually reinforcing HRM system.

1 The HRM strategies for resourcing in its broadest sense (ie identifying the skills and competences required), employee relations and human resource development flow from the business strategy. Both business and HRM strategies are affected by the internal and external environments.

2 Resourcing strategies indicate the skills and standards of performance required and are therefore linked with performance management and human resource development systems and programmes.

3 Performance management provides a basis not only for directly improving individual and, therefore, corporate performance, but also for rewarding people differentially according to the results they achieve and defining their training and development needs.

4 Resourcing, performance management, reward management, human resource development and employee relation activities combine to impact on performance levels.

Responsibility for HRM

It has been a constant theme in this book that HRM is owned and driven by top management, while line managers are responsible for its performance and delivery. HR professionals, however, still have a vital role in suggesting innovations and providing guidance and support. A cohesive and consistent approach to HRM is most likely to be achieved if the HRM function plays an active part in advising on and prompting the development of the principle HRM strategies and policies, as well as assisting in their implementation.

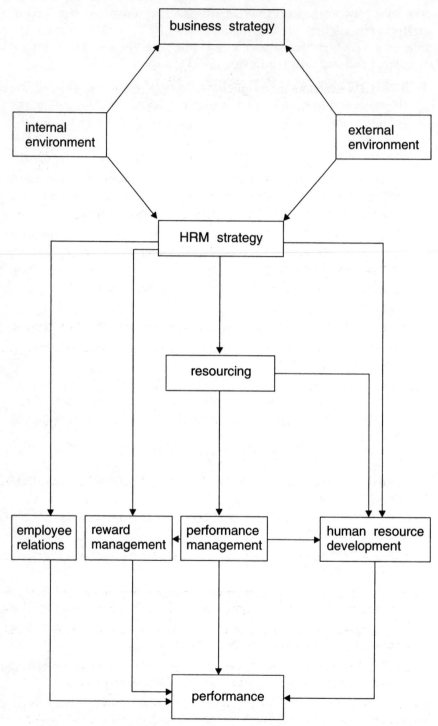

Figure 17.1 *The HRM process*

Bibliography

Armstrong, M (1987) 'Human resource management: a case of the emperor's new clothes?', *Personnel Management*, August.

Armstrong, M (1989a) *Personnel and the Bottom Line*, Institute of Personnel Management, London.

Armstrong, M (1989b) 'Personnel directors' view from the bridge', *Personnel Management*, October.

Armstrong, M and Murlis, H (1991) *Reward Management*, Kogan Page, London.

Argyris, C (1957) *Personality and Organisation*, Harper & Row, New York.

Atkinson, J (1984) 'Manpower strategies for flexible organisations', *Personnel Management*, August.

Atkinson, J and Meager, N (1986) *Changing Patterns of Work: How Companies Introduce Flexibility to Meet Changing Needs*, IMS, Falmer, Sussex.

Bales, R (1956) *Interaction Process Analysis*, Addison-Wesley, Reading, Mass.

Bandura, A (1986) *Social Boundaries of Thought and Action: A Social Cognitive Theory*, Prentice-Hall, Englewood Cliffs, NJ.

Barnard, C (1938) *Functions of the Executive*, Harvard University Press, Cambridge, Mass.

Beattie, D F and Tampoe, M K (1990) 'Human resource planning for ICL', *Long Range Planning* 23.1.

Beckhard, R (1969) *Organisation Development: Strategy and Models*, Addison-Wesley, Reading, Mass.

Beer, M (1984) 'Reward systems', in M Beer, B Spector, P R Lawrence, D Quinn Mills and R E Walton, *Managing Human Assets*, The Free Press, New York.

Beer, M, Spector, B, Lawrence, P R, Quinn Mills, D and Walton, R E (1984) *Managing Human Assets*, The Free Press, New York.

Beer, M, Eisenstat, R A and Spector, B (1990) 'Why change programs don't produce change', *Harvard Business Review*, November–December.

Beer, M and Spector, B (1985) 'Corporate transformations in human resource management', in R E Walton and P R Lawrence (eds) *HRM Trends and Challenges*, Harvard Business School Press, Boston.

Belbin, M (1981) *Management Teams: Why They Succeed or Fail*, Heinemann, London.

Bennis, W (1960) *Organisational Development*, Addison-Wesley, Reading, Mass.

Bevan, S and Thompson, M (1991) 'Performance management at the crossroads', *Personnel Management*, November.

Buchanan, D (1987) 'Job enrichment is dead: long live high performance work design', *Personnel Management*, May.

Buchanan, D and Huczynski, A A (1985) *Organisational Behaviour*, Prentice-Hall, Englewood Cliffs, NJ.

Burns, J M (1978) *Leadership*, Harper & Row, New York.

Burns, T and Stalker, G (1961) *The Management of Innovation*, Tavistock, London.

Cannell, M (1992) 'Teamworking – Lessons from the clothing industry', *Human Resource Management Yearbook*, A P Services, London.

Cannell, M and Woods, S (1992) *Incentive Pay: Impact and Evolution*, Institute of Personnel Management, London.

Chandler, A (1962) *Strategy and Structure: Chapters in the History of American Industrial Enterprise*, MIT Press, Cambridge, Mass.

Collard, R (1989) *Total Quality: Success Through People*, IPM, London.

Collard, R (1992) 'Total Quality and the human resource function', *Human Resource Management Yearbook*, A P Services, London.

Cooke, R and Armstrong, M (1990) 'Towards strategic HRM', *Personnel Management*, December.

Coopey, J and Hartley, J (1991) 'Reconsidering the case for organisational commitment', *Human Resource Management Journal*, Spring.

Cross, M (1991) 'Monitoring multiskilling: the way to guarantee long-term change', *Personnel Management*, March.

Cyert, R M and March, J G (1963) *A Behavioural Theory of the Firm*, Prentice-Hall, Englewood Cliffs, NJ.

Donovan Commission (1968) *The Royal Commission on Trade Unions and Employers' Associations*, HMSO, London.

Drucker, P F (1955) *The Practice of Management*, Heinemann, London.

Drucker, P F (1988) 'The coming of the new organisation', *Harvard Business Review*, January–February.

Emery, F E (1980) 'Designing socio-technical systems for "greenfield" sites', *Journal of Occupational Behaviour*, vol 1.

Fiedler, F (1967) *A Theory of Leadership Effectiveness*, McGraw-Hill, New York.

Fletcher, C (1984) 'What's new in performance appraisal?', *Personnel Management*, February.

Fombrun, C J (1983) 'Strategic management: integrating the human resource system into strategic planning', *Advances in Strategic Management*, vol 2, JAI Press, Greenwich, Conn.

Fombrun, C J, Tichy, N M and Devanna, M A (1984) *Strategic Human Resource Management*, John Wiley, New York.

Foulkes, F K (ed) (1986) *Strategic Human Resource Management. A Guide for Effective Practice*, Prentice-Hall, Englewood Cliffs, NJ.

Fowler, A (1987) 'When chief executives discover HRM', *Personnel Management*, January.

French, W R, Kast, F E and Rosenzweig, J E (1985) *Understanding Human Behaviour in Organisations*, Harper & Row, New York.

Giles, E and Williams, R (1991) 'Can the personnel department survive quality management?', *Personnel Management*, April.

Goold, M and Campbell, A (1986) *Strategies and Styles: The Role of the Centre in Managing Diversified Corporations*, Blackwell, Oxford.

Guest, D E (1987) 'Human resource management', *Journal of Management Studies*, 24.5.

Guest, D E (1989a) 'Personnel and HRM: can you tell the difference?' *Personnel Management*, January.

Guest, D E (1989b) 'Human resource management: its implications for industrial relations', in J Storey (ed) *New Perspectives on Human Resource Management*, Routledge, London.

Guest, D E (1990) 'Human resource management and the American dream', *Journal of Management Studies*, 27.

Guest, D E (1991) 'Personnel management: the end of orthodoxy?', *British Journal of Industrial Relations*, June.

Goold, M and Campbell, A (1986) *Strategies and Styles : The Role of the Centre in Managing Diversified Corporations*, Blackwell, Oxford.

Handy, C (1984) *The Future of Work*, Blackwell, Oxford.

Handy, C (1989) *The Age of Unreason*, Business Books, London.

Harvey-Jones, J (1988) *Making it Happen*, Collins, Glasgow.

Hendry, C and Pettigrew, A (1986) 'The practice of strategic human resource management', *Personnel Review*, vol 15, no 3.

Hendry, C and Pettigrew, A (1990) 'Human resource management: an agenda for the 1990s', *International Journal of Human Resource Management*, vol 1, no 1, June.

Herzberg, F W (1968) 'One more time: How do you motivate your employees?' *Harvard Business Review*, January–February.

Herzberg, F W, Mausner, B and Snyderman, B (1957) *The Motivation to Work*, Wiley, New York.

Humble, J (1970) *Management by Objectives in Action*, McGraw-Hill, Maidenhead.

Hunter, J E and Hunter, R F (1984) 'Validity and utility of alternative predictors of job performance', *Psychological Bulletin*, 96(1).

IDS (1986) 'Changing working practices', *Industrial Relations Review and Report* no 316, Incomes Data Services, London.

IRS (1990) 'Change to cell based working: multiskilling and teamworking at Digital Equipment VLSI', *IRS Employment Trends*, 475, November.

Janis, I (1972) *Victims of Groupthink*, Houghton Mifflin, Boston, Mass.

Johnson, G (1987) *Strategic Change and the Management Process*, Blackwell, Oxford.

Kanter, R M (1984) *The Change Masters*, Allen & Unwin, London.

Kanter, R M (1989) *When Giants Learn to Dance*, Simon & Schuster, London.

Keep, E (1989) 'Corporate training strategies', in J Storey (ed), *New Perspectives on Human Resource Management*, Blackwell, Oxford.

Kenney, J and Reid, M (1988) *Training Interventions*, IPM, London.

Kotter, J D (1980) 'What leaders really do', *Harvard Business Review*, May–June.

Latham, G P *et al* (1980) 'The situational interview', *Journal of Applied Psychology*, 65.

Lawrence, P (1985) 'The history of human resource management in American industry', in R E Walton and P R Lawrence (eds), *HRM Trends and Challenges*, Harvard Business School Press, Boston.

Lawrence, P and Lorsch, J (1967) *Organisation and Environment*, Harvard University Press, Boston.

Legge, K (1978) *Power, Innovation and Problem Solving in Personnel Management*, McGraw-Hill, Maidenhead.

Legge, K (1989) 'Human resource management: a critical analysis', in J Storey (ed), *New Perspectives on Human Resource Management*, Routledge, London.

Lewin, K (1951) *Field Theory in Social Science*, Harper & Row, New York.

Likert, R (1966) *New Patterns of Management*, McGraw-Hill, New York.

Litwin, G H and Stringer, R A (1968) *Motivation and Organizational Climate*, Harvard University Press, Boston, Mass.

Lowry, P (1990) as reported in *Personnel Management Plus*, December.

Mackay, L and Torrington, D (1986) *The Changing Nature of Personnel Management*, Institute of Personnel Management, London.

Mangham, L L (1979) *The Politics of Organisational Change,* Associated Business Press, London.

Marginson, P (1989) 'Employment security in large companies: change and continuity', *Industrial Relations Journal*, 20.

Maslow, A H (1954) *Motivation and Personality*, Harper & Row, New York.

McGregor, A and Sproull, A (1991) 'Employer labour use strategies: analysis of a national survey', *Employment Research Paper* no. 83, Employment Department, Sheffield.

McGregor, D (1957) 'An uneasy look at performance appraisal', *Harvard Business Review*, May–June.

McGregor, D (1960) *The Human Side of Enterprise*, McGraw-Hill, New York.

Miles, R E and Snow, C C (1978) *Organisational Strategy, Structure and Process*, McGraw-Hill, New York.

Miles, R E and Snow, C C (1984) 'Designing strategic human resource systems', *Organisational Dynamics*, Summer.

Miller, E and Rice, A (1967) *Systems of Organisation*, Tavistock, London.

Miller, P (1983) 'Strategic industrial relations and human resource management – distinction, definition and recognition', *Journal of Management Studies*, no 24.

Miller, P (1989) 'Strategic HRM: what it is and what it isn't', *Personnel Management*, February.

Mintzberg, H (1973) *The Nature of Managerial Work*, McGraw-Hill, New York.

Mintzberg, H (1981) 'Organisation design: fashion or fit?', *Harvard Business Review*, January–February.

Mintzberg, H (1983) *Power in and Around Organisations*, Prentice-Hall, Englewood Cliffs, NJ.

Mintzberg, H (1987) 'Crafting strategy', *Harvard Business Review*, July–August.

Moses, J L and Byham, W C (1977) *Applying the Assessment Centre Method*, Pergamon, Oxford.

NEDO (1986) *Changing Working Patterns*, National Economics Development Office, London.

NEDO (1991) *Introducing Teamworking in the Clothing Industry*, National Economics Development Office, London.

Ouchi, W G (1981) *Theory Z*, Addison-Wesley, Reading, Mass.

Owens, W A (1976) 'Background data', in M D Dunnette (ed), *Handbook of Industrial and Organisational Psychology*, Wiley, New York.

Pascale, R T (1990) *Managing on the Edge*, Viking, London.

Pascale, R T and Athos, A G (1981) *The Art of Japanese Management*, Simon & Schuster, New York.

Pava, C (1985) 'Managing new information technology: design or default?', in R E Walton and P R Lawrence (eds), *HRM Trends and Challenges*, Harvard Business School Press, Boston.

Pedler, M, Boydell, T and Burgoyne, J (1989) 'Towards the learning company', *Management Education and Development*, vol 20, 1.

Peters, T (1988) *Thriving on Chaos*, Macmillan, London.

Peters, T and Austin, N (1985) *A Passion for Excellence*, Collins, Glasgow.

Peters, T and Waterman, R (1982) *In Search of Excellence*, Harper & Row, New York.

Pettigrew, A (1976) 'The creation of corporate culture', Paper delivered in Copenhagen.

Pettigrew, A and Whipp, R (1991) *Managing Change for Competitive Success*, Blackwell, Oxford.

Pollert, A (1988) 'The flexible firm: fiction or fact?', *Work Employment and Sources*, 2.

Porter, L Steers, R. Mowday, R, and Boulian, P (1974) 'Organisational commitment, job satisfaction and turnover amongst psychiatric technicians', *Journal of Applied Psychology*, vol 59.

Porter, M (1985) *Competitive Advantage: Creating and Sustaining Superior Performance*, Free Press, New York.

Purcell, J (1989) 'The impact of corporate strategy on human resource management', in J Storey (ed), *New Perspectives on Human Resource Management*, Routledge, London.

Quinn Mills, D (1985) 'Planning with people in mind', *Harvard Business Review*, July–August 1985.

Rowe, K H (1964) 'An Appraisal of Appraisals', *Journal of Management Studies*, March.

Salancik, G R (1977) 'Commitment and the control of organisational behaviour and belief', in B M Staw and G R Salancik (eds), *New Directions in Organisational Behaviour*, St Clair Press, Chicago.

Saville, P, Nyfield, C, Sik, G and Hackston, J (1991) 'Enhancing the person–job match through personality assessment', Paper presented at the A P A Conference, San Francisco.

Saville, P and Sik, G (1992) 'Personality questionnaires: current issues and controversies', *Human Resource Management Yearbook*, A P Services, London.

Schein, E H (1969) *Process Consultation: Its Role in Organisation Development*, Addison-Wesley, Reading, Mass.

Schein, E H (1984) 'Coming to a new awareness of organisational culture', *Sloan Management Review*, Winter.

Schein, E H (1987) *Organisation Culture and Leadership*, Jossey-Bass, New York.

Schmitt, N, Gooding, R Z, Noe, R A and Kirsch, M (1984) 'Meta-analysis of validity studies published between 1964 and 1982 and the investigation of study characteristics', *Personnel Psychology*, 37.

Smith, M (1984) *Survey Item Bank*, MCB Publications, Bradford.

Smith, M (1988) 'Calculating the sterling values of selection', *Guidance and Assessment Review*, 4(1).

Stewart, V (1983) *Change: the Challenge for Management*, McGraw-Hill, London.

Storey, J (1987) 'Developments in the management of human resources: an interim report', *Warwick Papers in Industrial Relations* no 17, IRRV School of Industrial and Business Studies, University of Warwick.

Storey, J (1989) 'From personnel management to human resource management', in J Storey (ed), *New Perspectives on Human Resource Management*, Routledge, London.

Storey, J (1992) 'HRM in action: the truth is out at last', *Personnel Management*, April.

Storey, J and Sisson, K (1989) 'Limits to transformation: Human Resource Management in the British context', *Industrial Relations Journal*, 20.

Strebler, M (1991) 'Biodata in selection: issues in practice', *IMS Paper* no 160 Institute of Manpower Studies, Brighton.

Thomason, G F (1976) *A Textbook of Personnel Management*, Institute of Personnel Management, London.

Tichy, N M, Fombrun, C J and Devanna, M A (1982) 'Strategic human resource management', *Sloan Management Review*, Winter.

Top Pay Unit (1990) *Putting Pay Philosophies into Practice*, Incomes Data Services, London.

Torrington, D (1989) 'Human resource management and the personnel function', in J Storey (ed), *New Perspectives in Human Resource Management*, Routledge, London.

Townley, B (1989) 'Selection and appraisal: reconstructing social relations?', in J Storey (ed), *New Perspectives in Human Resource Management*, Routledge, London.

Trist, E L (1963) *Organisational Choice*, Tavistock, London.

Tuckman, B (1965) 'Development sequences in small groups', *Psychological Bulletin*, 63.

Tyson, S and Fell, A (1986) *Evaluating the Personnel Function*, Hutchinson, London.

Ungerson, B (1974) 'Assessment centres: a review of research findings', *Personnel Review*, Summer.

Vroom, V H (1964) *Work and Motivation*, Wiley, New York.

Walton, R E (1985a) 'From control to commitment', *Harvard Business Review*, March–April.

Walton, R E (1985b) 'Toward a strategy of eliciting employee commitment based on policies of mutuality', in R E Walton and P R Lawrence (eds), *HRM Trends and Challenges*, Harvard Business School Press, Boston.

Waterman, R (1988) *The Renewal Factor*, Bantam, New York.

Weick, K E (1977) 'Re-punctuating the problem', in P S Goodman and J M Pennings (eds), *New Perspectives in Organisational Effectiveness*, Jossey Bass, San Francisco.

Wickens, P (1987) *The Road to Nissan*, Macmillan, London.

Wickham, J (1976) 'Translator's introduction' in C Offe, *Industry and Inequality*, Edward Arnold, London.

Williams, S (1991) 'Strategy and objectives', F Neale (ed), *The Handbook of Performance Management*, IPM, London.

Wood, S (1992) 'Performance related pay', *Human Resource Management Year Book*, A P Services, London.

Wright, V C (1991) 'Performance-related pay', in F Neale (ed), *The Handbook of Performance Management*, IPM, London.

Yeandle, D and Clark, J (1989) 'Growing a compatible IR set up', *Personnel Management*, July.

Young, D (1992) 'Change and the personnel manager', *Human Resource Management Yearbook*, A P Services, London.

Author Index

Subject Index